HARWOOD HILL FARMS and Riding Ga

James J. Francis

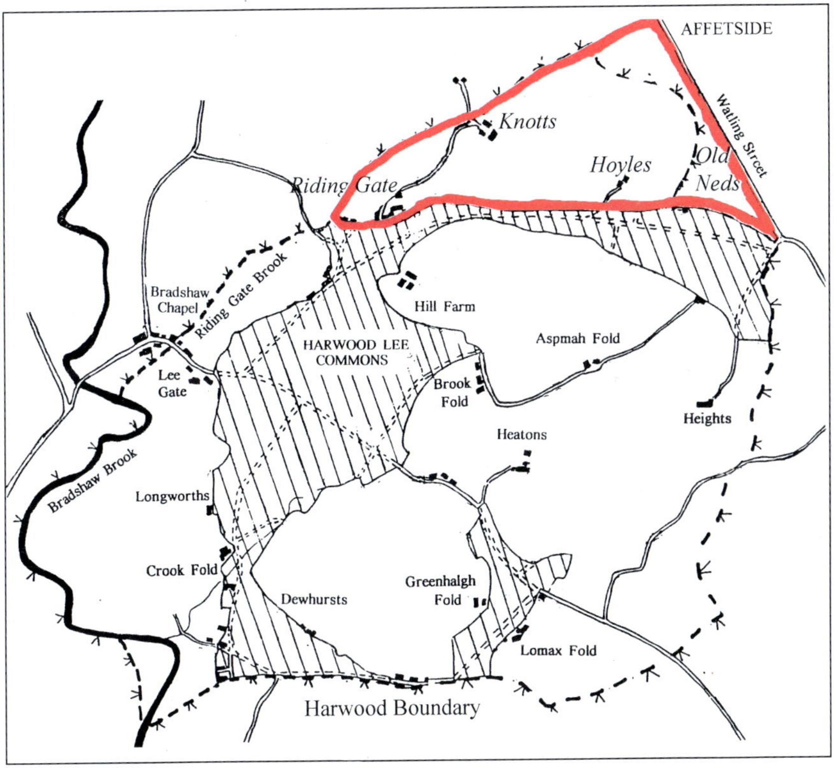

AFFETSIDE
Watling Street
Knotts
Hoyles
Old Neds
Riding Gate
Bradshaw Chapel
Riding Gate Brook
Hill Farm
Aspmah Fold
HARWOOD LEE COMMONS
Lee Gate
Brook Fold
Heights
Heatons
Bradshaw Brook
Longworths
Crook Fold
Dewhursts
Greenhalgh Fold
Lomax Fold
Harwood Boundary

Publication No. 25

September 2004

No 25 Harwood Hill Farms and Riding Gate
James J Francis

Published by Turton Local History Society, September 2004

ISBN 1-904974-25-2

TURTON LOCAL HISTORY SOCIETY

Turton Local History Society exists to promote an interest in history by discussion, research and record. It is particularly concerned with the history of the old Urban District of Turton, Lancashire and its constituent ancient townships of Bradshaw, Edgworth, Entwistle, Harwood, Longworth, Quarlton and Turton.

This publication is the twenty fifth issued by the Society. A list of previous publications is given on the inside front cover.

Meetings of the Society are held from September - May inclusive beginning at 7.30 pm on the third Tuesday of the month at the Barlow Institute, Edgworth. Visitors are welcome.

CONTENTS   PAGE

IILLUSTRATIONS

ILLUSTRATIONS (continued)

AUTHOR'S NOTE

This study was initially based on the Lever/Haslam documents (1595 - 1886) focusing on the three Knott's farms of Harwood. It soon became apparent however, that although in the neighbouring Township of Bradshaw, Old Ned's tenants were from the same families as those in the Knott's farms and had at one time had the same tenant for both.

It also became obvious that the early Riding Gate originated from the cottages built and owned by Top o'th' Knotts and that a study of the Knott's Estates naturally incorporated the development of Riding Gate as we know it today.

Because of these historic connections and the inter-relationships it seemed logical to incorporate the background history of the whole of the area within this publication.

Chapter I   THE KNOTTS FARMS OF HARWOOD   1600-1670

The north-western area of the Township of Harwood bounded by the Township of Bradshaw and Riding Gate Brook, stretching from Brookbottom Farm in the south-west to Old Ned's Farm in the north-east, is loosely referred to as the Knotts. This area has been defined from the 14th Century, being surrounded on the west, north and east by Bradshaw Township and the common land of Great Harwood Lee to the south.

The name Knotts is derived from the Old Norse 'Cnotts' meaning hill and the study area is in Harwood on the hill-side stretching up towards Affetside. Knotts land varies between 700 ft and 850 ft above sea level.

The Knotts area has been enclosed within recorded history and from the early 1600s has been made up of three separate holdings which up to 1603 were in the occupation of Henry Haworth, William Haslam and Matthew Harrison and now described as Top o'th' Knotts (West), Top o'th'Knotts (East) and Hoyles Fold, respectively. The total acreage of this area was approximately 66 Cheshire Acres, the measure used at this time and equivalent to 142 Statute Acres.

The earliest lease record of one of these holdings is dated 1607 from Sir Nicholas Moseley to Elizabeth Haslam, the widow of William Haslam deceased, who was buried at Bolton Parish Church on 23rd February 1603. The widow Elizabeth Haslam lived with her son Robert Haslam who had been baptised at Bolton Parish Church on 25th May 1595. Unfortunately place names were rarely noted in these early documents other than *'the said messuage or tenement in Harwood'*. However, later records place this holding as the Top o'th' Knotts Farm (East).

On May 1st, 1612, the Moseley Manor of Harwood - a little over half of the area of Harwood Township was sold for £1,100 to a group of five Harwood yeomen: Matthew Harrison, Henry Haworth, Raufe Higson, Lawrence Horrocks and Edward Greenhalgh. This sale was conditional that these Trustees would convey the various holdings to their occupants if they so chose, each to pay *'a proportional part of the purchase money if so minded'*.

It is interesting to note that two of the five Trustees lived in this northeastern corner of Harwood, namely Matthew Harrison and Henry Haworth. We have no record of Matthew Harrison's purchase but Henry Haworth bought his holding on 21st December 1613 from the other four Trustees for £160. The Haworth holding was simply described as *'All that messuage or tenement in Harwood now or late in the occupation of Henry Haworth'*. From a later deed of 1620 we can identify this original holding as Top o'th' Knotts Farm (West). However, before this purchase, Henry Haworth had married his neighbour, the widow Elizabeth

1

Haslam and his purchase from the Trustees would have included both the Top o'th' Knotts farms, East and West. Robert Haslam, now stepson of Henry Haworth, married Marie Astley, daughter of Gilbert Astley of Turton, Clerk - probably the Curate of Turton Chapel - at Bolton Parish Church on 6th November 1614.

As was customary with the more well-to-do marriages, portions were offered by the bride's father while the bridegroom's father was expected, in return, to give some security for both the bride and any resultant children. In this case a lengthy Marriage Settlement Agreement was concluded on 4th April 1620 between Henry Haworth, stepfather of Robert Haslam and four Trustees acting on behalf of the bride's father Gilbert Astley.

In consideration of £120 paid by Gilbert Astley to Henry Haworth as the marriage portion of Robert and Marie Haslam, Henry Haworth conveyed his estate to the four Trustees - Thomas Astley of Livesey, gentleman; Christopher Horrocks of Turton, gentleman; James Nuttall of Dedwayeclough, gentleman and Richard Wood of Turton, gentleman. There were various conditions of occupancy but after the deaths of Henry Haworth and his wife Elizabeth, all the estate would devolve to Robert Haslam and his heirs 'for ever'. If Robert and Marie Haslam had only daughters, then these daughters should eventually receive a 'portion' and an annuity of £10 per year for up to 14 years. Should Robert re-marry then the first son would be the heir to his estate.

The holding then in the occupation of Henry Haworth was to remain for the use of Henry and his wife Elizabeth rent free for six years or to the 'longer liver of them'. This holding was the original tenancy of Henry Haworth before his marriage to Elizabeth Haslam, widow. They also retained proportional commons rights. The field names were given and included Higher Carr, Lower Carr, Greaves, Lowmost Rydinge, Middlemost Rydinge, Limed Rydinge, Wald Rydinge, Little White Rydinge, New Close, Green Gate, Knotts, Lower Filcroft, Higher Filcroft, Rye, Calliade and Garden, Swine Orchard, Heighthill Acres, Rough Meadow, Green Fence and Brones.

Henry and his wife Elizabeth had the liberty to use the 'kilne and ovenhouse' with one moiety of 'housing with fire house over the hearth wall abutting towards northwest with the chambers over them'. They had the use of the Higher Barn and the byre in the Great Barn called the 'old wainhouse'.

Other parts of the holding were allotted to Robert and Marie Haslam including two parts of housing and barn with liberty of the fold (yard/lane area) and fields named as Rye Highfield; Roughing Bank; Lower Hanging Bank; Little Hanging Bank; Calfeheye; Another Calfeheye; Wife's Piece; Holt; Hill Meadow and Calfe Croft.

2

It seems that Henry Haworth and his wife Elizabeth occupied Top o'th' Knotts Farm (West) and Robert Haslam and his wife Marie occupied Top o'th' Knotts Farm (East), the latter being the earlier Haslam holding from at least the beginning of the 1600s.

It was agreed that Robert Haslam had the power to get coal from the one coal pit and stone from the stone pit. This (1620) is the earliest recorded evidence of a coal mine in Harwood. Robert could also sink new coal pits throughout the two farms, paying compensation to Henry Haworth for damage and trespass where necessary. Henry Haworth however could take stone as well as timber for necessary building work and could have coal from Robert Haslam for their *'necessary firing and fuel'.*

Elizabeth, wife of Henry Haworth died and was buried at Bolton Parish Church on 31st December 1621. Henry died the year after and was also buried at Bolton Parish Church on 26th May 1622. His will of 12th February 1622 was proved on his death and his Inventory appraised on 26th May 1622.

Although in the previous property Indentures Henry Haworth is described as a yeoman, in his Will he describes himself as a mason. From details of his debts owing and owed he notes payments to Richard Wood of the *'Oak'* and *'Bernard Wood for the work at the West Bridge at Sharples'.* This suggests he operated as contracting mason as well as a farmer.

Apart from leaving his estate to his stepson and heir Robert Haslam, Henry Haworth also left Robert two suits of clothes he had lent him, the standing bed, a chest of drawers, *'the chest and arke wherein all the evidence of this house are kept'* (the deeds) and *'the gold chain given me for serving the Churchwarden'.*

Henry Haworth specified many minor bequests including a brown heifer and a sidesaddle to Alice Berry, wife of Henry Berry. He gave his servant William Greenhalgh his bed and other furniture as well as £20. He made £5 bequests to Alice Warburton's children, £20 to his sister Alice Nuttall and £20 to his nephew John Nuttall as well as £20 each to grandsons Edward and David Nuttall. To Bernard Wood he bequeathed his best doublet with silver buttons and black fabric. To John Sharples he left his lined cloak and £20. His winter boots went to Henry Prescot. He gave to nephew William Liptrott his best gloves and £10 and to all the children to whom he stands as Godfather 17 pence apiece. Henry gave his servant Katherine Morris 12s.6d and the wheel (spinning). To John Haslam he gave a doublet and a pair of breeches while Henry Aferam of Edgworth received his silver dagger and William Bradshaw the great chair.

The rest of his goods, chattels and debts he bequeathed to *'Henry Darrow also Haworth'* - could this have been his illegitimate son?

Henry Haworth's inventory, appraised (valued) by James Jaques, Laurence Brownlowe, Edmond Wood and John Crompton is most interesting and gives a good picture of a yeoman farmer in 1622.

The most valuable item in the inventory were two oxen worth £9, while two mares and two horses were valued at £3 each. He had nine cattle, three calves and nine sheep. There were three saddles, a plough, pitchforks and other farming tools.

There are later references to the *'Great House'* and the furniture listed matches a house of this description. He had five beds, one being *'a standing bed with curtaines'* (four poster). Four chests were valued at 47s.4d while a table, two forms, a chest and a cupboard were worth 42s.6d. Pewter and brass items at £4.3s.11d and Henry Haworth's apparel at £6.2s.2d. All the items were listed and valued, even *'Dung and Manure'* at 20s. The total valuation was £105.2s.7d.

It seems that Robert Haslam and his wife Marie moved to live in the *'Great House'* after the death of their step father Henry Haworth because a deed of 5th December, 1630 details the sale to William Crompton, yeoman, of Breightmet for £160 of the holding Robert and Mary had previously occupied i.e., Top o'th' Knotts (East) also referred to at a later date as *'Houghs'* - possibly after a sub-lessee tenant.

This holding was described as *'All that little house standing on the south side of the Great House with all the chambers thereunto belonging'*. The great barn on the south side of the fold - one bay of which was to remain in the ownership of Robert Haslam, one little house standing at the west side of Middlemost Meadow near to Affetside. The fields were named and tied up with those detailed in the Marriage Settlement of 1620 with minor changes such as *'Wife's Piece'* now named 'Missys'.

The Rights of Common for this holding went with the purchase by William Crompton, as did all other rights and responsibilities. These would include mineral rights but as no mention is made of existing coal pits we can assume the only local coal mines at this date are within the Top o'th' Knotts (West) holding.

The holding that eventually became known as Hoyle's Fold was owned by Matthew Harrison when he bought it from his four fellow trustees after 1614. However one part of this holding was sold on 13th June 1634 by William Harrison to John Higson, yeoman of Harwood for £220. This sale included the messuage tenement and land in Harwood containing 21 acres previously in the occupation of Matthew Harrison, late father of William Harrison and now in joint occupation of John Higson and William Harrison but after the conveyance to be for the sole use of John Higson. Rights of Common were included.

On May 22nd, 1639 in the 14th year of King Charles I, Robert Haslam and William Haslam his son, with William Crompton conveyed the holding previously contracted to William Crompton - the Top o'th' Knotts (East) to Ralph Platt of Rumworth for £270. It would appear that the sale of 5th December, 1630 was not finally completed and the Haslams had retained part ownership - hence the tripartite partnership sale to Ralph Platt. As before the property conveyed did not include one bay of the barn. However the following March 1st, 1640, Robert Haslam, now described as a gentleman, and his son and heir William Haslam sold to Ralph Platt, a tanner of Rumworth for £3, the *'One bay of building to the south-east end of the barn of the said Ralph Platt'* - probably the *'old wainhouse'* referred to in the 1620 Marriage Settlement. This sale was conditional on an annual *'rent of one pig born at the Feast of the Pentecost yearly if it be lawfully demanded'*. Later documents refer to a peppercorn rent.

We have no record of changes during the Commonwealth period of Cromwell, but on the restoration of King Charles II to the throne, Top o'th' Knotts (East) was bought by the Lever family in whose hands it remained for the next two hundred years. This occurred on 2nd February, 1660 when Josph Platt of Rumworth, a yeoman, sold his holding to Thomas Lever of Chamber and his son Nathan Lever both designated as gentlemen, for the sum of £360. This was described as the property late in the holding of Ralph Platt (who bought it in 1639).

'All that little house standing on the south side of the Great House with all the rooms and chambers thereunto belonging - together with one upper chamber over the Great House in the north adjoining the little house, the Great Barn on the south side of the fold, one dwelling house at the west side of Middlemost Meadow nearunto Affetside, one swinehouse in the little fold, a garden and moiety of the Fold'. The fields were noted as Middlemost Meadow, Furthest Meadow, Great Highfield next to the Higher Barn, Rye High Field, Higher Hanging Bank, Lower Hanging Bank, Little Hanging Bank, Lower Kilne Croft, Great Calfhey, Missies, Park, House Fell Meadow, Fell Meadow Head and Hanging Bank - totalling 20 acres.

Thomas Lever was a member of the ancient Lever family of Bolton, who at this time were Lords of one quarter of the Manor of Great Bolton and lived at Chamber Hall, just to the west of the town on the River Croal.

The 21 acre holding bought by John Higson in 1634 changed hands again in 1662 when on September 14th Thomas Bridge, yeoman of Harwood with his wife Alice - daughter of the late John Higson - sold the holding to Thomas Lever of Chamber, gentleman, for £100. This Indenture refers to *'One messuage or dwelling house with appurtanences in Harwood wherein the said Thomas Bridge now inhabiteth'*. The old barn, the lower barn and one other messuage or dwelling house called the higher house, barn, garden and foldstead *'as is now marked and staked out or bounded'* - implying that a larger holding was being split up. Fields are named as Great Broome, Lower Broome, Little Broome, Great Croft otherwise called the Field towards Haslams and the Wood under the same, Half Acre, Rye Field, Field at the Door and Field above the Well, totaling 15 acres (Cheshire) being 8 acres of land (tilled), 2 acres of meadow and 5 acres of pasture.

This Indenture agrees that Thomas Bridge and his wife Alice may continue to occupy the holding if they pay Thomas Lever £6 on 1st September, 1662 and the sum of £106 on the 1st September, 1664 at which date on payment Thomas Lever will convey the property back to Thomas and Alice Bridge. This could be said to be an early short-term mortgage arrangement. The planned re-payment did not take place but Thomas Bridge and his wife Alice continued to occupy the holding on lease at £12.13s.4d per annum up to 1674.

From 2nd February 1667, Thomas Bridge also leased from Thomas Lever at £10 per year for three years the holding that had previously been in the occupation of Ralph Platt - Top o'th' Knotts (East). This lease document included the condition that Thomas Bridge should not plough more than three acres in any of the three years. He was also responsible for putting in repair and keeping in good repair all the houses, out-houses, hedges, fences and ditches and being responsible for paying *'all the leyes, hearth money, taxation and impositions whatsoever imposed or due for the premises to Church, King, Lord, Highways or otherwise due in anywise during the said term'*.

On 2nd April 1669, Thomas Bridge, his wife Alice and John Bridge son and heir apparent of Thomas and Alice sold to Thomas Lever of Chamber for £40 a holding *'heretofore in the occupation of John Higson deceased late father of Alice Bridge and now in the occupation of John Bridge'*.

This holding included one messuage or dwelling house, one barn, garden and fold and several closes of land named Higher Field, New Close and the Heath, totaling six acres. This was made up of three acres of land (tilled), one acre of meadow and two acres of pasture. All Rights of Common were included. Thomas and Alice Bridge signed with their *'mark'* while son John Bridge could sign his full name.

This purchase by Thomas Lever completed his ownership of all the land between Old Neds boundary and that of Top o'th' Knotts (West). These included the purchase from Joseph Platt in 1660 of Top o'th' Knotts (East) of 21 acres, the purchase from Thomas Bridge in 1662 of a 15 acre holding and later also from Thomas Bridge in 1669 a holding of 6 acres.

These latter two holdings made up what was to form Hoyle's Fold Farm of 21 acres.

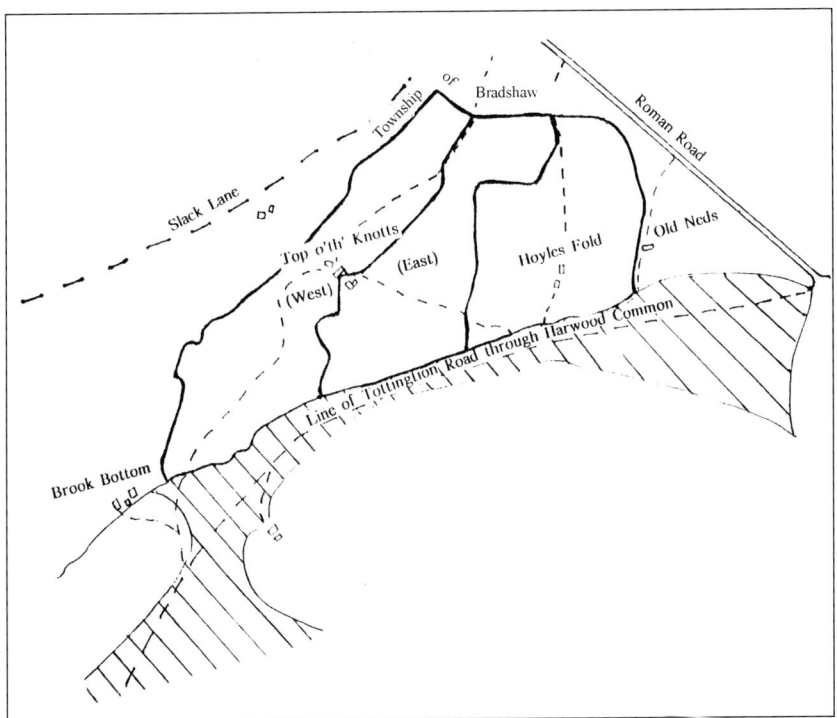

Tenants		Owners		
	1600	1620	1635	1670
Top o'th'Knotts (West)	Henry Haworth	Henry Haworth	Robert Haslam	Robert Haslam
Top o'th'Knotts (East)	William Haslam	Henry Haworth	William Crompton	Thomas Lever
Hoyles Fold	Matthew Harrison	Matthew Harrison	John Higson	Thomas Lever

Figure 1 List of Tenants and Owners of the Knotts Farms.

7

FIELD NAMES AND TOTAL ACREAGES OF THE KNOTTS FARMS
(As recorded in the 1600s)

Top o'th' Knotts (West)   Top o'th' Knotts (East)

Coal Pit Field   Middlemost Meadow
Higher Bent   Furthest Meadow
Barn Field   Great High Field
Ackers   Higher Field next to Higher Barn
Bent   Rye Highfield
Pickel   Higher Hanging Bank
Kill Bank   Lower Hanging Bank
Higher Green Glade   Little Hanging Bank
Lower Green Glade   Lower Kiln Croft
Lime Field   Great Calf Hey
Lower Lime Field   Little Calf Hey
Great Way Riding   Missies
Coal Pit Croft & Higher Meadows   Park
Lower Meadow   Fell Meadow
Hal Field   Fell Meadow Head
Thomasson Meadow   Hanging Bank
Graves

Statute Acres 51.2.10   Statute Acres 42.2.0
Cheshire Acres 24.0.12   Cheshire Acres 20.0.0

HOYLES FOLD
Old Barn
Lower Barn
Great Broome
Little Broome
Great Croft (also called the Field towards Haslams)
Half Acre
Rye Field
Field at the Door
Field above the Well
Higher Field
New Close
Heath

Statute Acres 44.1.24
Cheshire Acres 21.0.0   NB 1 Cheshire Acre = 2.12 Statute Acres

By 1670, the ownership of the three constituent farms was set to continue for the next 200 years. Top o'th' Knotts (West) continued to be owned by the Haslam family while Top o'th' Knotts (East) and Hoyles Fold were owned by the Lever family. This pattern lasted until the 1880s.

The Haslams farmed their holding of Top o'th' Knotts (West) as well as operating their coal pits. Top o'th' Knotts (East) and Hoyles Fold were on the other hand leased out to tenants for farming only while some coal mining was carried out independently.

We know that Hoyles Fold was leased to Thomas Bridge for a further two years in 1672 at £12.13.4. per year when it was described as *'the messuage and lands whereupon Thomas Bridge now inhabiteth'*. We have no further record of the Bridge family at Hoyles but there were Bridges at neighbouring Old Neds until the early 1700s.

On 1st January 1670, Top o'th' Knotts (East) was leased jointly to John Hough and Robert Haslam, owner of Top o'th' Knotts (West), initially for a term of eleven years at £11 rent per year. This farm was referred to as *'Houghs'* on a later plan of the early 1800s. The lease was conditional on keeping the houses and outhouses in good repair as well as the Upper House towards Affetside. They were expected to pay all taxes *'to Church, to King and Highways'*. The owner, Thomas Lever, retained the right to sink and operate coal pits and to fell timber.

This lease for Top o'th' Knotts (East) must have continued as John Hough died there on 6th February, 1713 and his Will (made 1698) refers to having given several sums of money as marriage portions to Robert Haslam on his marriage to John Hough's daughter Elizabeth. John Hough, after providing for his wife Margaret, left the remainder to his daughter Elizabeth Haslam and afterwards to their children.

The inventory of John Hough's estate was valued at £33.4.0. including a young red cow at £3.10.0, two other cattle at £4.15.0. and a bay mare valued at £3.15.0. There were two carts and a pair of wheels, two harrows, a plough and horse gear, etc, one swine, hay and corn. The house seemed well furnished with a great table, cupboard, seated and other chairs, two beds, arks and stools, brass and pewter and a clock valued at ten shillings.

In 1744, a John Haslam, as well as being the tenant of Hoyles was recorded in the Bradshaw Estate Rent Rolls as also leasing the neighbouring farm of Old

Neds. He was followed by James Haslam, possibly John's son as tenant of Hoyles while a Thomas Haslam continued as tenant of Old Neds to the end of the 1700s.

The Bolton Archives hold an original copy of a *'Chapman's Accounts'*, covering the second half of the 1700s. These were the merchants traveling around the locality buying, selling and supplying goods to the farmsteads by packhorse. An entry in the accounts of 30th August 1781 details a delivery of hops (2lbs) and malt (1/4 load) at 1s.6d and 14s.6d respectively to James Haslam of *'Oyles'*. There were other small deliveries of hops in September and December 1781, so we can assume that they were brewing their own ale for home consumption. The derivation of the name 'Oyles' *or* 'Hoyles' cannot be traced, but this 1781 record has been the first to be found.

Coal mining appears to have been continued on a small scale by the Haslams in the northern part of their Top o'th' Knotts (West) farm, but little is recorded until the 1800s by which time the coal mining was undertaken by professional mining operators with the Haslams receiving rentals on their coal rights.

This pattern was also taken up by the Lever family but certainly in the first half of the 1700s they undertook their own mining operations.

An agreement dated 27th November, 1738 details a shaft-sinking contract sited in Fell Meadow of Top o'th' Knotts (East). This contract between Samuel Lever (the then owner) and Edmund Lomas of Tottington with James Holt of Bradshaw, both described as coal miners, was to sink a rectangular shaft of 6ft 4ins by 4ft 6ins down to coal, which was about 100ft deep. They were also to drive a water drainage level from this shaft to the 'Old Pit' at the top of Fell Meadow. The payment agreed was fifteen shillings per yard depth of the shaft and one shilling and eight pence per yard for the water drainage drift.

Coal mining must have continued in this area to their northern boundary with Bradshaw Township illustrated by a legal arbitration agreement between Thomas Lever (the then owner) and James Haddock of Edgworth and Joshua Haslam of Tottington dated 27th February 1765. The parties were bound to (accept) the arbitration ruling on the fine of £500. Thomas Lever had made complaints of trespass and damage by the operators of the neighbouring coal mine in Bradshaw (Messrs Haddock and Haslam) to the Lever coal pit in Harwood. The result of the arbitration is not known, but the coal mining must have been highly valued for the parties to be bound by the arbitration sum of £500.

The coal mining in the area, coupled with farming, led to increasing requirements for colliers, leading inevitably to housing requirements for these workers. The earliest mining activities being on the Affetside ridge probably encouraged the development of cottages along Watling Street. In the 1630 sale of Top o'th' Knotts (East) to William Crompton, *'one little house standing on the west side of Middlemost Meadow near Affetside'* was included in the transfer - this could well have been the nucleus for the later development of the Swine Trough cottages on the Top o'th' Knotts (West) land to the east of the farm houses which appear to have been built c1750 by the Haslam family and remained in the Knotts estate until bequeathed to members of the family by Robert Haslam's Will of 1809.

The Swine Trough cottages were built adjacent to the lane leading to Affetside in the southerly corner of Coal Pit Field - suggesting why they were built here, to house the colliers of the adjacent coal pits.

Similarly, several cottages had been built in Riding Gate by the Haslams on the north side of the brook and remained within the Knotts estate until dispersed to the family by the Will of John Haslam of 1784.

The name of Riding Gate appears to refer to the way or entrance to Great Harwood Lee (common land) from the Great Way Riding - the largest field of the Top o'th' Knotts (West) farm. Another 'gate' named after a field was 'Redman Gate' at the end of Watling Street, named after the Redman field of Old Ned's.

It seems clear from the Enclosure Awards and Map of 1797 that north of Riding Gate Brook there were at this time only cottages built and owned by the Haslams of Top o'th' Knotts (West). On the south side was the group of buildings developed by the Entwistles, the first record of which is the Will of John Entwistle dated 18th April 1759. John Entwistle, after various bequests, left a cottage to each of his sons, John Jnr. Richard and Ralph. These constituted the earliest of the Old Green group and the current owner justifiably considers that these cottages were developed from an earlier cottage, stable and shippon of the early 1700s.

It is difficult to draw up a family tree of the Haslams but our first record of this branch of the family was of William Haslam of Top o'th' Knotts (East) who died in 1603. His widow Elizabeth married her neighbour Henry Howarth of Top o'th' Knotts (West) who left his Knotts estate to his stepson Robert Haslam who was born in 1595. Robert married Marie Astley in 1614 and they had a son William who was recorded in 1640. Few records exist for the following fifty years but William's grandson, Robert Haslam married Elizabeth Hough in 1697. Their son John Haslam died on 3rd May 1784, having made his Will on 2nd October 1780.

It seems that up to this time Top o'th' Knotts (West) covered the same area as described in the early 1600s, i.e. all the land and property north of the Riding

Gate Brook between Brookbottom Farm on the west, the Bradshaw boundary to the north and Top o'th' Knotts (East) boundary to the east. The later Enclosure Map, however, details two small extensions of one perch each of the common land north of the Riding Gate Brook.

Although several cottages were built in Riding Gate and at Lower Knotts they were at this time part of the Top o'th' Knotts (West) estate owned by John Haslam up to 1784. However, by his will some of the Riding Gate cottages were bequeathed to members of his family. By examining the Enclosure Awards Map of 1797 and a subsequent estate map, a picture of the early Riding Gate hamlet can be seen to emerge.

John Haslam appears to have married the widow Mary Hamer on the death of his first wife Isabel with whom there were four sons, Robert, Nathaniel, Thomas and John and two daughters, Betty who married James Hamer, husbandman of Bradshaw, and Mary who married an Ormrod.

On John Haslam's death on 3rd May, 1784, his Knotts estate was left to his son and heir Robert Haslam with the exception of nine cottages in Riding Gate which were bequeathed; three to son Nathaniel, one to son Thomas, one to Nathaniel's son William and four to trustees (Parson James Folds and George Bradshaw of Brookbottom) who were empowered to let or sell these four cottages and the rents or profits to go to son John and his heirs.

There were various charges to the Knotts estate to pay for bequests made by John Haslam to his daughters while the lease he had on the neighbouring Crompton Farm in Bradshaw was passed to his son Robert. One other cottage, probably adjacent to the farmhouse, was bequeathed to his servant Alice Butler for her life.

As no specific bequests of coal mining profits were made we can assume that all coal rights remained with the Knotts estate under the heir Robert Haslam and at this time there appeared to be no mining under Riding Gate.

In common with several townships within the Parish of Bolton-le-Moors, the freeholders of Harwood felt that greater efficiency of land use and some personal benefit would result from the Enclosure of Harwood Commons. The first meeting to discuss this matter was held at the 'Horse Shoe Inn' in Bolton on 3rd September 1781. It took a further sixteen years to sort out local differences and the final *'Act for Dividing, Allotting and Inclosing the Commons and Waste Grounds within the Township of Harwood'* was enacted by Parliament in 1797. Amongst the influential land/property owners of Harwood who initiated and finalised the Inclosure were Robert Haslam and Robert Lever.

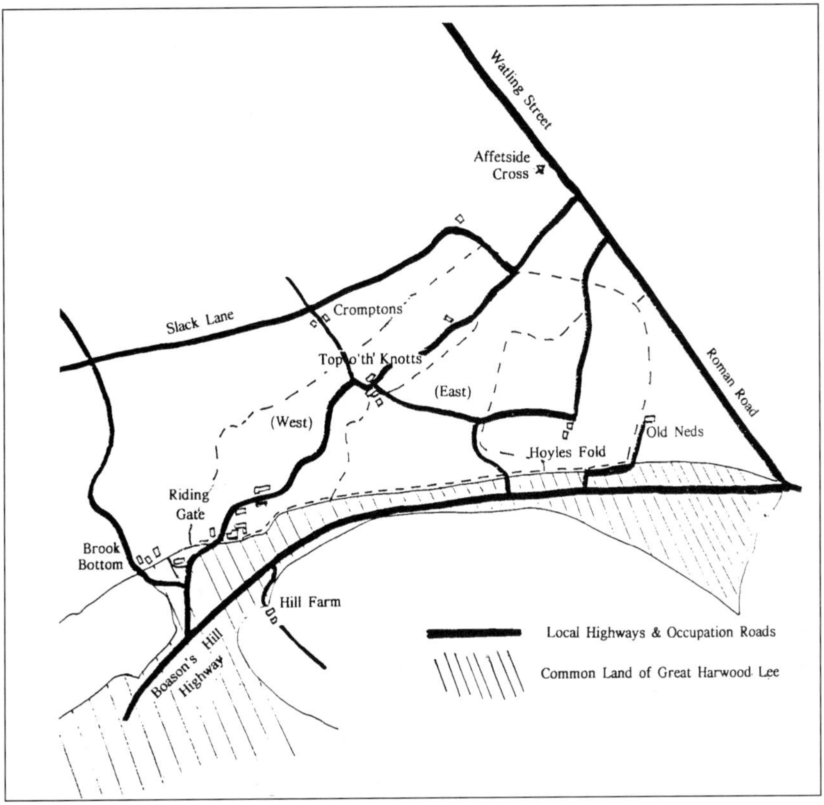

Figure 2 Road system in the Riding Gate and Knotts area of Harwood - 1790

Legend on map:
Watling Street
Affetside Cross
Slack Lane
Cromptons
Top o' th' Knotts
(East)
(West)
Old Neds
Hoyles Fold
Riding Gate
Brook Bottom
Hill Farm
Roman Road
Boason's Hill Highway

Local Highways & Occupation Roads
Common Land of Great Harwood Lee

A Plan
of the
Commons
and Waste Lands within the
Township of Harwood
with the Allotments Divisions and Roads thereof
as laid down by the Commissioners appointed by an Act passed
in the 37th Year of his present Majesty's Reign.
R. Fletcher. 1790 and 1801.

13

The Commissioners appointed were James Brandwood of Edgworth, Richard Aspindell of Great Bolton and Ralph Fletcher of Haulgh whose duty was to administer the final Awards of Allotments after deciding on the roads to be made and the various occupation roads and footpaths to be defined. The areas of the allotments were directly proportional to the value of the freeholds and where possible were allotted adjacent to their existing freeholds or elsewhere by agreement.

The Lever family estate including Top o'th' Knotts (East) and Hoyles Fold entitled them to allotments of land between the new Boasons Highway (Tottington Road) and the Riding Gate Brook from *Dearn Style* (near Raikes Farm) up to Redman Gate with a total area of 8 acres.2r.16p, most of which was adjacent to their two existing farms.

Robert Haslam, based on his freehold of Top o'th' Knotts (West), was allotted a total of 13 acres.2r.6p. He had three separate allotments; one of 4 acres.3r.39p alongside Boasons Hill Highway on which the Grey Mare Inn and Pawsey Bank were later built; one of 8 acres.1r.34p on the southerly side of Riding Gate adjacent to Top o'th' Knotts (West) and a small piece of one perch on the north side of the brook up to Brookbottom boundary.

Other qualifying freeholders in the area included James and Ralph Entwistle of Old Green who were allotted pieces of land on the east side of the new road into Riding Gate. Michael Howarth who owned the cottages, now known as Top o'th' Brow had a small piece adjacent to his cottages and another piece on Boasons Hill Highway, and Oliver Ormrod who owned Hill Farm was allotted a piece of land on the corner of the lane leading to Brookbottom, while Henry Isherwood had the piece opposite up to Old Green.

Of the other freeholders of Riding Gate, all were recipients of the late John Haslam's bequests of 1784. Nathaniel Haslam for his three cottages and his son's cottage was allocated 1 acre.0r.4p on the east side of Riding Gate Lane and a small piece of one perch on the north side of the brook. Thomas Haslam for his cottage was allocated the small corner piece at the junction of Riding Gate Lane and Boasons Highway, now known as the 'Nook'. The four cottages in trust for John Haslam entitled his devisees to a piece of land of just over one acre where the Knowles Buildings and other adjacent cottages now stand. The new allotments in the Riding Gate area opened up further development of cottage property in the 1800s.

On the death of his father John, Robert Haslam as heir took over Top o'th' Knotts (West) and ran this farm along with the neighbouring farm of 'Cromptons', leased from the Bradshaw Hall Estate, then belonging to Thomas Isherwood. Robert must have decided to rebuild the old 'Great House' when the estate became his on his father's death in 1784, and a substantial farmhouse and cottage was re-built as one unit apparently on the footprint of the previous building, still being attached at the rear to the south-facing farmhouse of Top o'th' Knotts (East). To commemorate the rebuilding, Robert included a datestone with the inscription *'Robert and Mary Haslam, 1784'* carved in an oval with decorations carved in each corner spandrel. Examination of the stonework of the building suggests that the party wall between the two farmhouses was retained but with the new building increased slightly in height. The small section of the south facing rear wall clear of Top o'th' Knotts (East) farmhouse still has its original window opening with moulded drips. The style of the stonework supports this rebuilding theory in that the gable ends and north front wall above window height are laid in the later 'water-shot' style in regular and graded courses while below window height the stonework is in the older regular but rougher stone courses in common with the stonework of the Top o'th' Knotts (East) farmhouse. It seems that Robert Haslam re-used two of the old mullion windows with moulded drips on the north facing front elevation while fitting the flush faced lintels of the period for the other windows and doors.

Figure 3 Datestone of Robert and Mary Haslam on the rebuilt front wall of Top o'th'Knotts farmhouse.

Robert Haslam as owner of Top o'th' Knotts (West) continued to farm the holding with his second wife Mary until his death on 17th May 1809. His first wife, also Mary, had predeceased him and it appears she had been previously married as Robert in his Will left property to stepson John Hamer. As well as farming, the coal mining of the area had become well established.

In addition to the stepson, John Hamer, Robert Haslam had son Robert as his heir and a younger son James. He also had five daughters, Elizabeth Haslam, Mary Hamer, Rachel Heaton, Ann Ramwell and Margaret Ormrod. His daughter Alice who had previously died had been married to James Fletcher, an innkeeper of Sharples.

In Robert Haslam's Will of 12th April, 1809 he left to his widow Mary the use, for life, of the *'cottage at the end of the barn'* as well as the new cottage at Swine Trough and *'the bed and bedding in the parlour with the clock that was John Haslams'* and the household goods, furniture, *'spoons that were her own before marriage'* and £15 per year, charged to son and heir Robert, which had been *'secured by a marriage settlement of 9th September, 1795'*. His widow Mary was also to *'have a new black gown at my death'*.

Son and heir Robert Haslam received the freehold estate of Knotts with messuages, dwelling houses, etc, being charged with £200, the interest of which was to go to stepson John Hamer until his death when the £200 would revert to Robert.

To son James he left the newly erected property - occupied by Abraham Settle and Elizabeth Ormrod - on his Enclosure Award land known as Hogscar and including the part called the Raikes - this would constitute the holding now known as Raikes Farm on Tottington Road.

To stepson John Hamer, the deceased also left one of the other cottages at Swinetrough occupied by John Turner and *'all those cottage houses at Riding Gate now in the occupation of Richard Manchester, John Haslam, - Entwistle, Ann Grundy and Richard Scowcroft'*. There is no explanation as to where these are but were probably the group of cottages just over the bridge into Riding Gate. John Hamer also received the £50 loan Robert Haslam had made to the Little Bolton to Edenfield Turnpike Trust.

To grandson Oliver Ormrod he left the middle house at Swinetrough occupied by William Davenport and to his grandson John Ramwell, the third house at Swinetrough occupied by John Booth, This row of cottages at Swinetrough was situated on the old lane from Top o'th' Knotts to Affetside.

To his son-in-law George Heaton who had married Robert Haslam's daughter Rachel he left *'the land on which he has lately erected two dwelling houses and a shippon with a two yards privilege to rear for repairs'*. He was also given the right to get water from the Limed Meadow -*' the adjoining field, as well as the liberty to erect a privy on the fence'*.

These two dwelling houses *'lately erected'* have a datestone on the south facing wall of 1795 with George and Rachel Heaton's names. On the north facing back wall is a long line of mullioned window lights. These lights stretch behind both houses and would have allowed for a loom-shop of the period - a domestic workshop for handloom weaving. These two *'new'* houses appear to have been built on to a pair of older cottages, probably dating from the early 1700s.

Robert Haslam also left to his daughter Rachel Heaton *'a piece of land now in possession of George Heaton called Hill Nook'*. This appears to be the land on Tottington Road where the Hill Brow cottages were built. All Robert's daughters also received £20 each and equal shares of the household goods and chattels etc.

Robert Haslam, having died in 1809, also willed that his brother Thomas Haslam should retain one third of the coal mining rights under the Knotts estate with the other two thirds to be equally shared by his daughters Elizabeth, Mary and Rachel, and his grandchildren Ralph and Betty Fletcher. These owners of the coal mining rights or their representatives could sink and dig any pits, tunnels, etc, under Top o'th' Knotts (West) farm and get stone to make and repair roadways and had liberty to erect head-gears and engine houses, etc, as necessary. They were responsible for all mining expenses and rectifying damage, filling up disused shafts, etc. This mining partnership had to pay to heir Robert Haslam Jnr, one shilling per week as long as mining continued under the estate.

On the death of Robert Haslam, his personal estate and effects were valued at under £1,500.

Little is recorded of the coal mining activities at this time but later plans of the 1840s indicate a lot of mining on the southern part of Top o'th' Knotts estate.

Robert Haslam Jnr as heir to father Robert's estate in 1809 continued to farm and live at the Top o'th' Knotts (West) farm. In the 1841 Census Returns he was noted as a farmer of 80 years living with his children Anne aged 35, James of 35 years and Thomas 30 years of age.

Robert died four years later and was buried at the Bolton Parish Church on the 25th April 1845; the burial certificate quotes his age as 87 years, a discrepancy

Figure 4 Lower Knotts Cottages: the *'lately erected'* pair on left were built by George Heaton joining up with earlier cottages to right.

Figure 5 George Heaton's *'loom-shop'* houses showing the ornate datestone to him and his wife Rachel dated 1795.

Figure 6 The Lower Knotts Cottages (now Nos. 91 & 93) left to Peter Haslam by his father Robert in 1845. A 1914-18 War photograph with a son on leave from the army.

Figure 7 Top o'th' Greaves cottages built alongside the ancient roadway from Riding Gate to Top o'th' Knotts.

with the Census information but not unusual. He had made his Will on 27th June, 1836 and named his eldest son Robert as heir to his Knotts estate with certain exceptions and conditions defined, some very onerous, which must have placed the heir in a financially difficult position.

The deceased left his son Peter *'two dwelling houses with land as now fenced off situate in the Lower Meadow'*, occupied by John Smith and William Unsworth. The description places it as Nos. 91 and 93 Lower Knotts alongside the ancient occupation road to Top o'th' Knotts. The reference to *'as now fenced'* suggests they had been built in the recent past, probably c1800. By 1830 Peter Haslam had moved to take up the tenancy of Top o'th' Knotts (East) Farm from the Lever family.

To his son James Haslam, Robert left one dwelling house *'being part of the Knotts estate with a privilege of 3 yards ladder room at the rear for repairs, etc'* in the occupation of James Platt. A similar dwelling house with wall at front and the privilege of a 3-yard space at rear for repairs together with access to the front, in the occupation of Robert Heaton was left to son Thomas Haslam. The only other cottage property in the Knotts estate with a similar defined privilege of a repairing space at the rear were the two dwelling houses built by George Heaton in 1795 at Lower Knotts, suggesting these two houses left by the deceased Robert Haslam to his sons James and Thomas were the other two in the Lower Knotts group of four. The bequest of these four cottages to his sons completed the distribution to the family of all the Knotts cottage property apart from those in the immediate vicinity of the farm itself.

The deceased Robert Haslam left his daughter Ann Haslam his interest in the local Turnpike Trust and the bedroom furniture she had used while living at home. To his son James he also left 2/5 of two houses he owned in Little Bolton and to him and his brother Thomas he left the bedroom furniture they had used at home - provided they had remained at Knotts to his decease.

The heir Robert may have been farming elsewhere in his own right but the deceased directed that all farming stock, implements, and the remainder of his personal estate and effects be shared equally between all his children. The most onerous requirements on the heir Robert Haslam Jnr. however, were a series of cash settlements the deceased had made to his other children, all charged against the Knotts estate and payable within 12 months of his decease. There were £200 payments to daughter Mary, wife of Samuel Scowcroft, to daughter Alice, wife of Thomas Ormrod and daughter Ann. £120 to son Peter, £150 to son James, £150 to son Thomas and £190 to daughter Eliza, wife of Robert Crook. This total of £1,210 to be found in the first 12 months by the heir Robert Haslam Jnr. must have been a serious blow and probably led to the final demise of the

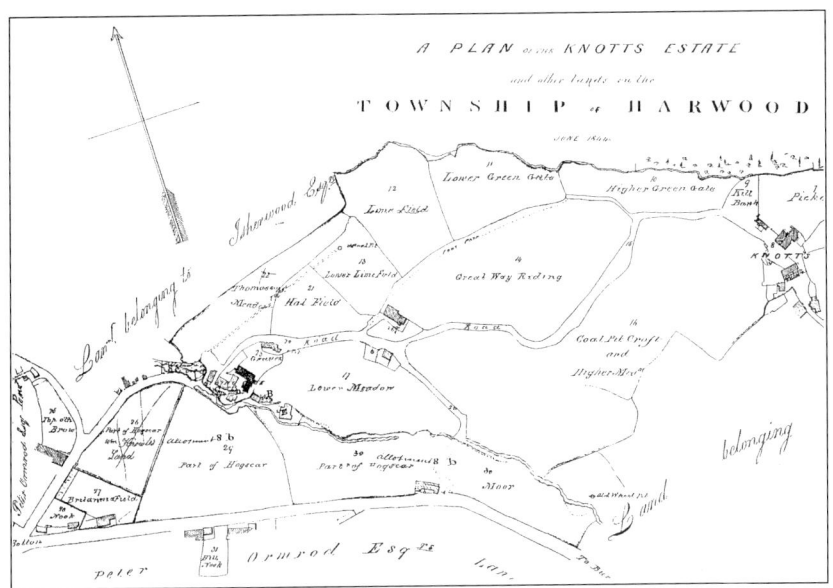

Figure 8 A Plan of the Knotts Estate in 1844: note field No 14 '*Great Way Riding*', possibly giving the name 'Riding Gate' as the 'way' or 'gate' to Harwood Common.

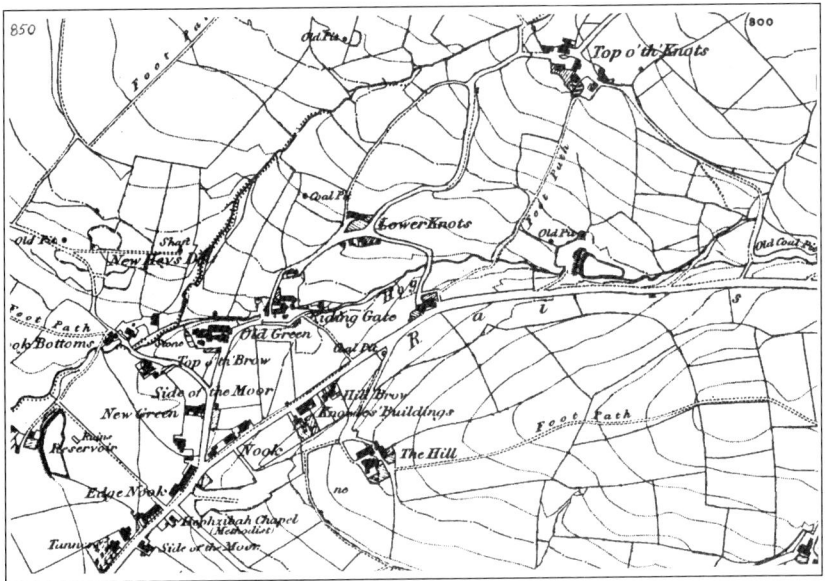

Figure 9 OS Map of Riding Gate and the Knotts area of Harwood - 1850

Haslam estate of Top o'th' Knotts (West). It is not known whether this money (about £600,000 by today's values) was paid over or whether the various sums remained as loans or shares in the estate, probably the latter. While leaving this financial burden on his son's shoulders, it may be interesting to note that the personal estate of the deceased was under £300.

The 1851 Census Returns noted the heir Robert Haslam as farming Top o'th' Knotts (West) of 22 acres (Cheshire measure) and employing two men. He was 56 years of age living with his wife Betty aged 57, daughter Margaret aged 27 and granddaughter Ann aged 7. An agricultural labourer named George Constantine aged 22 also lived in. A similar picture was noted in the 1861 Census with daughter Margaret described as a dairymaid but the granddaughter Ann lived elsewhere.

Robert Haslam died on 19th December 1863 aged 68 years followed by his wife Betty's death on 18th April 1869. Their son Robert had also died in 1863 aged 44 leaving no direct family succession. The father, mother and son were all buried in St Maxentius churchyard, Bradshaw Chapel.

Because there were no direct descendants to work it, the farm seems to have been leased out, by the Haslam family, until finally sold.

At the next Census of 1871, the farmer of Top o'th' Knotts (West) is noted as Mary Haslam, widow of 50 years of age with her son Robert aged 19, daughter Ellen of 15 years, Isabella aged 14 and another unnamed daughter of 13 years. Mary Haslam farmed 48 acres and employed two men. Her background is not known but after studying the various local marriage registers, it is possible she was previously Mary Howarth of Turton who married Thomas Haslam, son of a Bradshaw farmer on October 23rd, 1850 at Bolton Parish Church.

The 1881 Census also notes Mary Haslam as the farmer now 60 years old with her 29-year-old son Robert and daughter Ellen of 26, and a farm labourer John Isherwood aged 34 living in. Soon after this census Mary Haslam decided to retire and a sale of her stock was held at Top o'th' Knotts (West) on 21st September 1882. She died a few years later at Riding Gate and was buried on 7th November 1888 in St Maxentius churchyard.

Mary Haslam was succeeded as tenant of Top o'th' Knotts (West) by Robert Haslam her son aged 36 years. He was recorded as farmer here until 1894 when the tenancy was taken over by Elija Lonsdale who remained tenant until his death early in the 1900s.

Early 19th Century records are sparse for the Lever family who owned Top o'th' Knotts (East) and Hoyles Fold farms, except that Adam Green leased Hoyles during the early 1800s followed by Abraham Leach in the 1820s. It was during Abraham Leach's tenancy that he lost a cow which fell into Mr. Scowcroft's unfenced coal pit shaft known as Ladder Pit and he took the coal pit operator to court claiming damages in March 1828. This coal pit is on the Hoyles Fold side of Riding Gate Brook and being named as Ladder Pit would have had access by ladders to the workings below. The shape of the land occupied by the pit is still to be seen and fenced off with the enclosure land on the south side of the brook originally awarded to Thomas Jackson, the Lever family heir. This pit is also at the end of the culverted section of the Riding Gate Brook forming the road to Old Ned's Farm and to the Old Pit at the bottom of Old Ned's land. Apart from this Ladder Pit there are no other known pit shaft sites on Hoyles Fold land.

James Hamer took over Hoyles Fold tenancy after Abraham Leach in 1841 being aged 45 years living with his wife Mary also 45 and sons Joseph (15), James (14), Andrew (12); and daughters Hannah (10), Elizabeth (8), and Margaret (4). Living with them at the time of the Census was Elizabeth Horrocks of 64 years and described as independent. It is possible that James Hamer of Hoyles was related to John Hamer at Old Neds in 1841.

The Knotts estate of the Lever family had been passed down through the female line to the Jacksons since the late 1700s and rents were collected through a local land agent. An example of a half year's account/report by Edward Scott is recorded on 12th May 1838. Both James Hamer of Hoyles and Peter Haslam of Top o'th' Knotts (East) were paying £20 per year. John Nuttall (possibly from Old Pit higher up Tottington Road) paid £1 per year to get stone from the delph adjacent to Riding Gate Brook. There must have been a complaint against James Hamer, because he promised 'to spread all the manure which arises upon the land' while he was also 'desirous to have the old cottage repaired'; we assume this was not done and it was finally demolished.

By 1851 Charles Grime, aged 50, was the tenant farmer of Hoyles with his wife Betty of 45 years. They have no children noted but have two 'home servants', Alice Heathcote of 19 and Sarah Ratcliffe of 14 years. There is also a John G Horrocks noted as a visitor - of ? months! Charles Grime still farmed at Hoyles in 1861 with his wife. Sarah Ratcliffe is now noted as a power weaver and John Grime aged 11 as a boarder/scholar.

The 1871 Census records James Hamer aged 35 years as tenant of Hoyles but is described as a coal miner living with his wife Betty and their three daughters, Sarah Ann aged 10, a half timer at a factory, Mary aged 8 and Emma 2. Son Daniel was under one month old.

The 1880s saw ownership changes in both of the Lever/Jackson family farms of Top o'th' Knotts (East) and Hoyles Fold. The latter farm was purchased from the Jackson family in c1889 by Thomas Lowe. Thomas aged 56 years was noted as farmer with 58 acres and was a member of the Lowe family who were also farming at Bradshaw Head and Lower Nuttalls. Thomas Lowe died and was buried in St Maxentius churchyard on 18th November 1889, resulting in the 1891 Census noting his widow Margaret then aged 63 as farmer at Hoyles. After a family agreement of March 1894 between Thomas Lowe's five sons John, Thomas, James, Andrew and Alfred, it was decided that Alfred should take over Hoyles Fold as part of their family estate from their mother Margaret.

At the beginning of the 19th Century in 1805 the Land Tax Register noted Oliver Ormrod as tenant of Top o'th' Knotts (East) as well as being assessed for a coal mine; this record also applied in 1815 and 1825. The coal mine could well have been the pit in the Fell Meadow towards Affetside.

The tenant to follow Oliver Ormrod was Peter Haslam in the late 1820s. The Lever/Jackson rental accounts of 1838 note that Peter Haslam was paying £20 per year. In common with his neighbour James Hamer at Hoyles he complained about the condition of the property and Peter Haslam is reported by the agent Edward Scott as *'not willing to give any more rent - nor does he seem desirous to have the lease. He says the roof of his house is so bad he will give notice to leave unless it is repaired'.* Regardless of these threats Peter Haslam's family stayed at Top o'th' Knotts (East) until they bought the farm in c1880.

By the 1841 Census Peter Haslam aged 40 was noted as the farmer with his wife Sarah of 35 years and sons James 12, Thomas 5, Samuel 2, daughter Ann 9 and baby Elizabeth of one month. The Edwin Scowcroft Survey of Harwood in 1845/6 notes Peter Haslam as having 18 acres.3r.6p (Cheshire Measure) with a valuation of £44.15s.4d compared with Robert Haslam at Top o'th' Knotts (West) having 21 acres.1r.2p valued at £74.11s.8d.

By 1861 Peter's son James Haslam aged 32, had taken over the farm with his wife Elizabeth aged 24, daughter Ann aged 7, and sons Thomas aged 5 and Peter 2. Father Peter and his family had taken the tenancy of Meadowbarn Farm leaving eldest son James to farm Top o'th' Knotts (East). A memorial in St Maxentius graveyard records Peter Haslam's death at Meadowbarn on January 28th, 1884 aged 84, his wife Sarah having predeceased him in 1881. James Haslam continued as tenant farmer of 40 acres in 1871 with his daughter Ann, of 17 years, working as a finisher at a bleachworks and young Thomas, of 14 years, working at home. The rest of the family included younger sons, Peter 12 and Samuel 9, recorded as scholars, together with a younger brother, James aged 1, and a baby sister, under one month, and still unchristened.

Elizabeth wife of James Haslam died and was buried in St. Maxentius churchyard on 18th May 1874. James married again on 20th October 1875 to Lydia Woodward, a spinster of Longworth Township and daughter of William Woodward, a blacksmith. The 1881 Census records James Haslam now 52 years old as farmer of 40 acres with his new wife Lydia of 46, and son Peter aged 22 working on the farm. Son Samuel of 19 worked as a wheelwright's apprentice while James 12, Elizabeth 10 and Emma 7 were scholars - probably at the newly opened Affetside School.

The Lever/Jackson family sold off their last Harwood property c1880 when Top o'th' Knotts (East) was purchased by the tenant James Haslam who in the 1891 Census was confirmed as a 62 year old farmer with his wife Lydia while both son James and daughter Elizabeth worked on the farm.

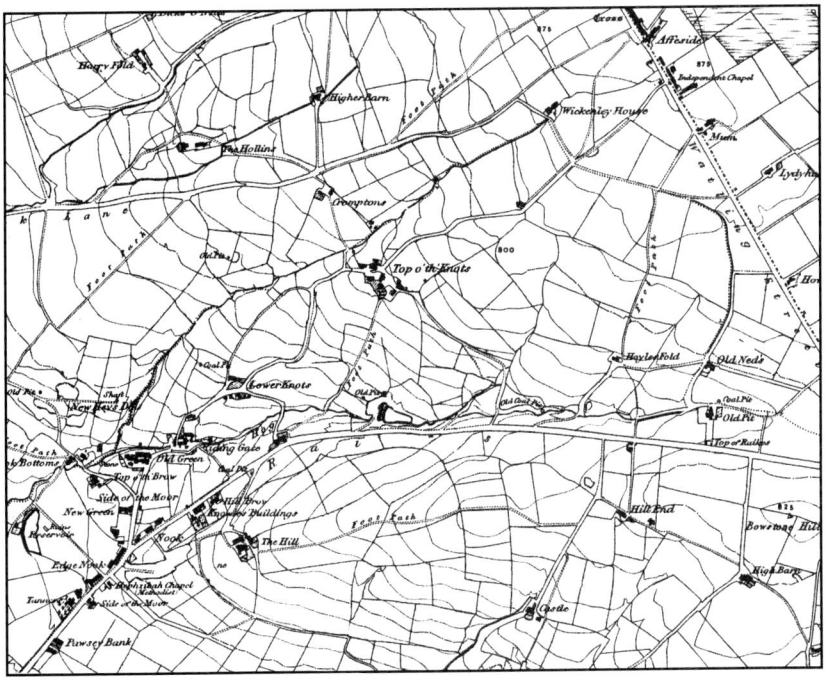

Figure 10 OS Map: 1850: Riding gate to Affetside, note Top o'th' Knotts, Hoyles Fold and Old Neds Farms.

Figure 11 Top o'th' Knotts (West) farmhouse north front in 2002, described as the *'Great House'* in early documents. This is the rebuild of 1784.

Figure 12 Top o'th' Knotts (West) farm buildings remaining after loss of the old barn in the fire of 1976.

Figure 13 Top o'th' Knotts (East) farmhouse in 2002: note difference in roof height and relative size.

Figure 14 Top o'th' Knotts (East) farm buildings in 2002

Figure 15 Hoyles Fold farmhouse.

Figure 16 Hoyles Fold farm buildings. Tottington Road to the right.

Chapter IV   BRIDGES; EDWARD BRIDGES OR OLD NEDS

Old Ned's farm sits in the triangle of land formed between the northeastern boundary of Great Harwood Lee, being part of Harwood Commons, and the ancient highway of Watling Street, from the Knott's estate at its southwest. Although the 'odd man out', being within the Township of Bradshaw rather than Harwood like its neighbouring Knott's farms, the close proximity led to common family ties of the tenants of both Knotts and Neds for hundreds of years.

Old Ned's was a farm within the Bradshaw Estate originally owned by the Bradshaws of Bradshaw. The earliest record of the Bradshaw farms was made in the Will of John Bradshaw in 1542 when he left to his heir sixteen messuages (a messuage is described as a house and the ground around it) so these could be farms, smallholdings or cottages with a garden.

In 1670 John Bradshaw sold off three farms to Thomas Smith of Smithfould, namely Walsh Fold, Brown Barn and Bradshaw Head farms.

Just before his death in 1694, John Bradshaw, the Lord of the Manor of Bradshaw, contracted to sell his manor to a distant relative, Henry Bradshaw of Marple Hall in Cheshire. The sale documents include references to '*messuages, tenements and cottages in Bradshaw now or late in the tenures or occupations of Thomas Hamer, John Walworth, Edward Bridge, John Hamer Snr, George Bradshaw, Thomas Bridge, John Hamer Jnr. John Bradshaw of Offside, Widow Greenhalgh, John Walch, John Brookes, John Bradshaw of Brookbottom, John Wood, Rauffe Tonge, Robert Farnworth, Hugh Bradshaw, James Ramsden, Thomas Settle, John Lomax, Alexander Bradshaw and John Nuttall'*, twenty-one in all.

Henry Bradshaw, the new Lord of the Manor, chose to remain living at Marple Hall and leased out Bradshaw Hall and the previous demesne lands along with all the other properties to tenants on various lease arrangements. The Rent Rolls include twenty-seven properties on lease of which sixteen pay a tithe as well as rent suggesting there are sixteen agricultural holdings. It is worth noting that up to this time there were no lands in Bradshaw outside the Bradshaw Estates, other than the three farms sold in 1670 and Birches Farm on a 999-year lease to Sir Robert Barton of Smithills.

In the 1600s there were Bridges farming in the Knotts estate who could well have been related to **Edward Bridge** of Old Neds.

The **Edward Bridge** Tenement is mentioned in the Will of John Hamer of Bradshaw dated 7th August, 1724: '*I will, give and bequeath to my son Richard his heirs and assigns Hardier Closes (fields on the Tottington side of Watling*

Street also belonging to the Bradshaw Estate) and all my right and title unto the tenement commonly called Edward Bridge Tenement'. This Will of 1724 suggests that Edward Bridge may have already left the farm before his death in October 1725.

The next detailed record is that of the Bradshaw Estate Rent Rolls covering the period 1728-1753. The **Edward Bridge** holding is noted as paying £1.3s per year rent and 2s.11d for commuted tithes. This farm is referred to as *'Edward Bridge Tenement'* in 1732 and *'Late Bridges'* in 1739. In 1742 the rent is paid by John Barlow for *'Bridge Tenement'* and in 1744 by John Haslam for *'Hoyles Tenement'*, still paying £1.3s per year rent and 2s.11d tythes. We know from our Knotts studies that John Haslam was also renting Hoyles at this time which is the neighbouring farm to Old Neds (Bridges).

The Harwood Commons Enclosure Act of 1797 had no effect on Old Neds being in Bradshaw, but it did affect its access road. The Enclosure Plan details *'Old Neds Gate'* on the southerly occupation road leading to the old road along the culverted Riding Gate Brook in the Harwood Common. After the enclosures, Old Neds entry lane was closed and a new lane constructed leading to Watling Street in the northeast. The junction of Watling Street and the newly built Tottington Road was called Redman Gate - the entry to the Common from the Old Neds field called *'The Redman'*.

The next estate document noting *'Bridges'* is the Bradshaw Family Recovery Deed dated 15th August 1806 which notes *'Bridges'* in the occupation of Thomas Haslam and Ralph Pilling. Thomas Haslam was the brother of Robert Haslam owner of Top o'th' Knotts (West) and Ralph Pilling was probably the sub-lessee. The fields of *'Bridges'* are named as *'Meadow, Lower Close, Higher Close, Higher House Field, the Stope, the Great House Rough, the Acre* and *the Redman'* having a total area of 17 acres.2r.21p.

The Land Tax Assessment records from 1780 to 1830 show the Haslam family as tenants throughout the fifty years records and the name *'Old Neds'* was first referred to in 1798. Thomas Haslam was noted as occupier until 1812 followed by his son John until 1831.

In 1831, a survey and map was drawn up, by Thomas Bird, of the Bradshaw and Tottington estates belonging to John Isherwood Esq., then Lord of the Manor of Bradshaw. *'Neds'* is noted as 22 acres.2r.20p let at will at £38 per year to John Haslam. The fields are noted as Higher and Lower Meadows, Higher and Lower Redman Fields, the Acre, Higher and Lower Closes, Higher House Field and the Stopes. Although some of the earlier fields have been sub-divided, field names and those noted in the 1806 Recovery Deed confirm that Bridges and Neds are

Figure 17 Old Neds south facing front: house part to left, shippon and stable are outshuts to the barn.

Figure 18 Old Neds: north facing rear, outshut to house body cuts off original barn door lintel, stable lean-to on left of barn - 1968.

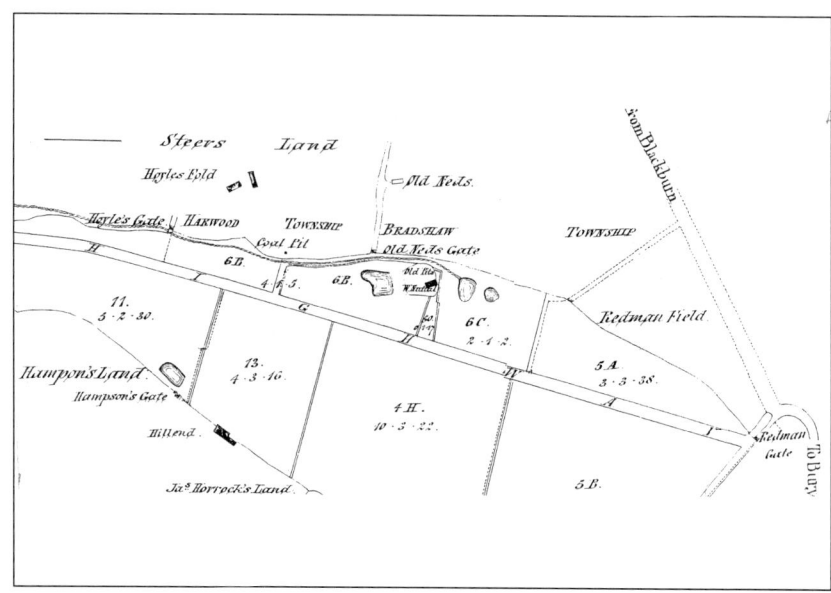

Figure 19 1797 Enclosure Map showing Hoyles Fold & Old Neds: note Old Neds gate & ancient road to Tottington Rd, both gates to the commons.

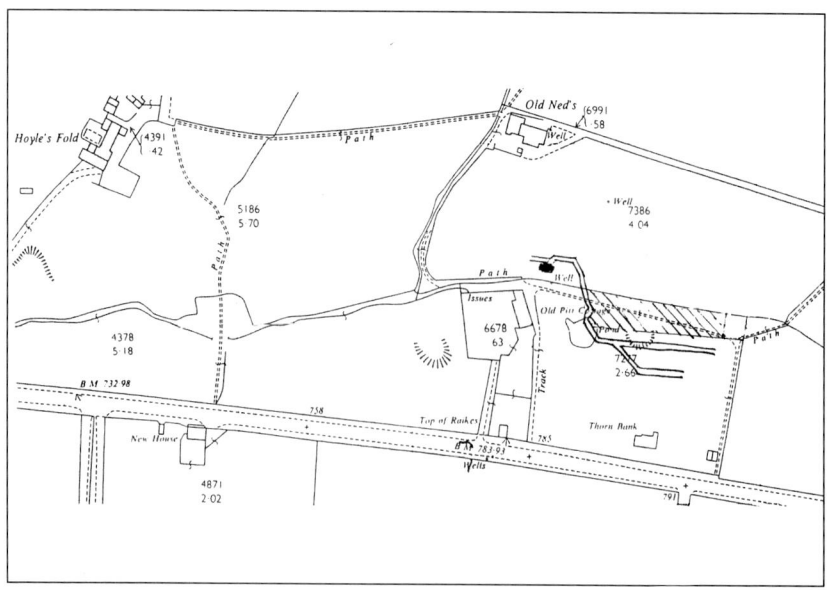

Figure 20 Current OS Map with workings connecting up to 180ft deep shaft in Old Neds land.

one and the same property. The acreages were likely to change as the tenancy was let at will by the landlord on a yearly basis.

Thomas Haslam died in 1812, his Will of 8th January 1808 bequeathed to his son John Haslam '*All my tenant rights, terms and interest in the farm in my occupation called Old Neds in Bradshaw subject to rent, covenants, and agreements reserved'*. Thomas also left to his son John '*my shares in coal in Harwood and share in headstocks, etc, subject to rents payable to brother Robert'*. This refers to the Haslam coal mining interests in Top o'th' Knotts (West) land.

Thomas had received cottage property under his father John's Will of 1784 which qualified him for an award of an allotment under the Enclosure Act and he left his son John his Enclosure Award at Riding Gate consisting of a parcel of land at the corner of Tottington Road and Riding Gate lane numbered No 41 and was of 38 perches area. This section of land included '*two cottages or dwelling houses lately erected thereon now in the occupation of my said son John Haslam and Richard Settle'*. With the remainder of this parcel of land he left his son John '*All the stone now got and being on the road side adjoining for the purpose of building thereon'*. This latter piece of the allotment and the stone eventually became 'The Nook' - with a date-stone of 1816 carrying the names of John Haslam and his wife Margaret. It is not known whether John Haslam continued to live at the Nook or at his tenancy of Old Neds, which he could have sub-leased.

Thomas Haslam also left his son John his Riding Gate cottages then occupied by James Haslam and James Ramsden as well as two other cottages bought from Oliver Ormrod occupied by John and William Collier and Michael Howarth and one fifth part of five cottages at Riding Gate occupied by John Haslam, Richard Scowcroft, Richard Manchester, William Entwistle and Ann Greenhalgh. The latter was probably Thomas's share of his father's bequest under trustees.

At the bottom of Old Neds 'Meadow' field near the line of the Riding Gate Brook forming the boundary of Bradshaw Township with Harwood Township is an old coal pit shaft, found quite accidentally by the author. This is shown on the 1845 OS Map as 'Coal Pit' and opposite is the Harwood property of 'Old Pit Cottages'. Their deeds refer to a 2000 year lease dated 15th February, 1723 between '*Thomas Bridge and James Heaton'* - this could have been a regularisation of trespass on to the Harwood Common. There is no reference in these deeds to the coal pit, and the property is described as a farmhouse and cottage with half an acre of land. The pit shaft is of rectangular form 7ft x 6ft and 180ft deep - with 80ft of water in it when opened up. The form suggests it could have been both a winding and pumping pit with an egress for water lifted into the adjacent Riding Gate Brook. No documentary information is available as to who operated the pit, or when, but a plan of 1843 shows coal workings in the Harwood field on the opposite side of the brook. The Enclosure Act of 1797 refers to the road leading to Old Pit Cottages and the Coal Pit *'now working'*. This plan is of *'Colliery Workings situate at Old Neddys'* in the working of Messrs Jackson and Fletcher. The Jacksons were the last descendants of the Lever family to own adjacent Hoyles Fold and Top o'th' Knotts (East) and this particular field was awarded to them under the Enclosure Act of 1797. The part marked as mined is noted as *'the Old Works and has been got by the Lessees of Bradshaw Colliery'*. Underground roads appear to have been driven under Old Neds field to connect up to the Old Neds shaft. It is interesting to note that in a Survey of Harwood dated 1845/6 made by Edwin Scowcroft, Old Pit is described as a house and barn with land of 4 acres.1r.13p in the occupation of John Nuttall with the added note *'Fletcher & Nuttall Colliery'*. Although no plans of this colliery exist, it is likely to have been worked from the 1750s to the 1860s.

In the Census of 1851, John Hamer is noted as the farmer of Old Neds with a son John then 24 described as a coal miner. Ten years later in the 1861 Census young John Hamer has taken over Old Neds from his father, who was then 81 years old, and is then described as a farmer as well as a coal miner. The Hamers succeeded the Haslams as tenants of Old Neds in the late 1830s and in the 1841 Census were noted as John Hamer and Alice his wife, each of 60 years of age with daughters Ellen aged 20, Alice aged 14 and son John aged 13. By 1851 son John Hamer is noted as a coal miner and daughter Ellen had married John Walker also a coal miner who lived with the family at Old Neds.

The 1861 Census describes son John now aged 33 as a farmer of 10 acres as well as being a coal miner. He and his wife Elizabeth aged 27 now had three children, Ellen aged 6, Alice aged 5 and infant John. Described as a retired farmer, old John Hamer and Alice his wife now both aged 81 still live with their family at Old Neds - all living in a two bed-roomed farmhouse.

In 1871, the Census notes John Hamer continuing as farmer with daughters Ellen (16) and Alice (13) working as cotton weavers. Young John of 10 years was a scholar joined by brothers William (4) and James (2). Their grandfather, John Hamer, now aged 90 years still lived with the family although his wife Alice had recently died. John Hamer continues as farmer of Old Neds in 1881, now 54 years of age with his wife Elizabeth of 47 years. Their unmarried daughter Alice of 22 is still working as a cotton weaver with 20 year old son John being a wheelwright apprentice. Son William of 14 is a cotton weaver while the younger James aged 11 and Elizabeth aged 6 are described as scholars - probably at the Affetside School. Daughter Ellen had married Baxter Entwistle, a 26 year old engine driver from Affetside, on January 15th, 1879 at St Maxentius Church, Bradshaw. Old John Hamer had however died aged 94 in October 1875 and was buried in St Maxentius graveyard.

Figure 21 Old Neds barn roof showing trusses and purlins - 1968.

Figure 22 Barn trusses preserved in bedroom wall - 1980.

Figure 23 Old Neds in renovated form - 1980.

Alice Hamer married William Walsh, a 26 year old packer of Higher Bradshaw at St Maxentius Church on June 1st, 1882 and left the family home. At the 1891 Census John Hamer aged 64 is still noted as farmer of Old Neds with his wife Elizabeth. John aged 30 and now a wheelwright is still at home with brother James aged 21, a plasterer, sister Elizabeth aged 16, a bleachworks worker and Maria aged 5. James married Ellen Hamer aged 29, who was a weaver living at Bradshaw Brow, at St Maxentius Church on May 6th, 1896. The schedule of properties in the Bradshaw Estate dated 19th November 1907 noted *'John Hamer, yearly rent of Old Neds with 23.138 acres at £25 per year'*. A year later a St Maxentius Parish Magazine noted *'Burial of John Hamer formerly of Old Neds Farm on November 13th, 1908 aged 82 years. His wife Elizabeth died in 1912 aged 77 years'*. From 1914 to 1916, Old Neds was tenanted by Zacharias Taylor who had moved from Edgworth.

The Bradshaw - Isherwood family, owners of the Bradshaw Hall Estates since 1694, decided in 1919 to sell all their properties in our area. The auction took place on December 4th, 1919 but Old Neds (23.124 acres) was sold prior to the auction on April 3rd, 1919 to Mr and Mrs John William Warburton of Raikes Cottage, Tottington Road, Harwood. Old Neds was noted as being occupied by Samuel Scowcroft.

After some renovations, cement rendering over the stonework and a new wall to the shippon, John Warburton sold Old Neds to William Merrills whose mortgage was revoked and the farm was re-possessed by J W Warburton in 1924. The farmhouse and one field of 4.215 acres was sold on September 12th, 1924 to Mr Edward and Eliza Jane Shaw, an iron moulder of Heapfold Farm, Bury, while the balance of Old Neds farm land was retained by the Warburton family and leased for use by neighbouring farms. Edward and Eliza Shaw additionally bought Smithy Meadow (3a.3r.3p. acres) in 1934 from W Z Seddon - this field was part of the Harwood Common awarded at the time of enclosure to Matthew Fletcher, the then owner of Height Farm. The Shaws established a poultry farm and latterly ran sheep and in 1935, to supplement the continuing water shortages, Teddy Shaw sank a 3ft diameter well fifty foot deep in their Close Field.

The author and his wife Joan bought Old Neds Farm with approximately eight acres of land in 1967 from Mrs Eliza Jane Shaw, widow of Teddy Shaw who had died in 1964. This acquisition and subsequent study of the property set off a life long interest in local history in conjunction with the Turton Local History Society. The farmhouse was renovated utilising the barn section for additional living quarters taking care that the ancient oak beams and trusses were preserved in situ. The land is still grazed by cattle coming through from Hoyles Fold, maintaining the several hundred years connection between Old Neds and the Knotts farms.

Chapter V   RIDING GATE - THE EARLY DAYS

Although we may call the whole area from Tottington Road to the end of the lane, Riding Gate, prior to the Enclosure of Harwood Commons in 1797 the name was limited to describe the group of approximately a dozen cottages on the north side of Riding Gate Brook only. The road leading from Top o'th' Knotts through Riding Gate was the 'way' or 'gate' to Great Harwood Lee common land over the brook from the Great Way Riding, the largest field of Top o'th' Knotts (West) farm. The only other property in the near vicinity were the cottages of the 'Green'. To the north of the Riding Gate group were the cottages along the old occupation road to Top o'th' Knotts known as the Greaves - named after the field of that name and the Lower Knotts cottages a little further to the north-east, the name indicating a position somewhat lower than the Top o'th' Knotts' farms.

Halfway down the lane to Brookbottom Farm was a group of cottages (only two initially) called Top o'th' Brow and on Tottington Road, then known as Boasons Highway or Raikes Lane near the entrance to Riding Gate Lane, there were several cottages and farm buildings named Edge Nook.

Up to the death of John Haslam of Top o'th' Knotts (West) in 1784, all the cottages and buildings to the north of Riding Gate Brook had been built by and belonged to the estate of Top o'th' Knotts (West). They were built from the early 1700s probably for the local colliers and handloom weavers.

The area between Riding Gate and Tottington Road was known as the 'Green' or 'Side o'th' Moor', the earliest development being by the Entwistle family on the 'Green' dating from the early 1700s. Initially a small farm with house, shippon and stable built by John Entwistle who later converted his buildings into three cottages which on his death in 1759 he left one to each of his sons, John Jnr, Richard and Ralph. By the time of the Enclosure of Harwood Commons in 1797, this group of cottages was owned by Ralph and John Entwistle.

The Top o'th' Brow cottages, built c1750 were at the time of the Enclosures owned by Michael Haworth.

On the westerly side of Riding Gate Lane towards the Tottington Road corner was a small holding with a building owned by John Brook. This bordered onto 'Hawkhurst', the farm of Henry Eskrick who had been the beneficiary of the Brook family estate originating with Brookfold in the 1600s. Henry Eskrick owned the buildings and cottages on the corner of Tottington Road built in the late 1700s.

Below these on the westerly side of Tottington Road was the grouping known as Edge Nook. They comprised of two three-storey cottages in the centre with a pair of two-storey cottages on each side. The northerly three were built by John Thweat in 1783, probably in conjunction with his diversion of Riding Gate Brook to form the reservoir for his new Lee Gate Bleachworks across the field. John Thweat had taken out the long lease of this piece of land in May, 1783 on which to build 'one or more good and substantial dwelling houses' and he covenanted to leave 'a three yards space at the rear for a public street' and the right to allow building on each gable end. On the same date in 1783, William Scowcroft, innkeeper of the 'Three Jolly Crofters' at Bradshaw Chapel took out a similar long lease to that of John Thweat for another piece of land at the southerly end of Thweat's land on which to build three dwelling houses. William Scowcroft also covenanted to leave three yards of his land to form a six yards wide street. Other buildings were later built to the rear, probably with access via their 'public street'.

The three cottages of John Thweat were taken over by Thomas Hardcastle as part of the absorption of the Lee Gate Bleachworks into the Bradshaw Hall Works in 1829 and eventually into the Bleachers' Association Ltd assets in 1901.

When John Haslam of Top o'th' Knotts (West) died in 1784 he left nine of his Riding Gate cottages to his sons. To Nathaniel he left three cottages now known as the Greaves, then in the occupation of James Lomax, Edmund Holt and Thomas Entwistle. The cottages directly below the Greaves were left to trustees the Rev James Folds and George Bradshaw in trust for son John Haslam who may have been at this time under age. These consisted of four cottages and two shippons in the occupations of James Thomasson, William Haslam, Richard Manchester and Thomas Entwistle. These locations seem to be confirmed by a legal agreement document in the possession of the Greaves owners where the dispute was over the ownership of the piece of land between the Greaves and the cottages below numbered 69, 71 & 73. An agreement was made 10th August 1797 to share the land equally between Nathaniel Haslam and his brother Thomas after the death of their brother John. This piece of land called the 'Backside' was defined as being of 16 perches area. A later map of 1844 confirms this piece as the Greaves of 16 perches area.

A single cottage in the occupation of John Thomasson was left to son Thomas Haslam. This was probably the cottage at the far end of Riding Gate alongside the stream and Thomas was given the liberty to build one further bay building onto the gable end, making up what are now Nos 77 and 79.

Grandson William, son of Nathaniel, was also left a cottage occupied by Widow Entwistle, which was probably on the brook side, long since demolished and replaced by privies and now garages.

These bequests by John Haslam on his death in 1784 distributed property to his family who were later able to benefit from the Enclosure Act of 1797 by qualifying for Awards of allotments of the Commons. The chart on page 43 describes the position of the various Awards in Riding Gate vicinity paving the way for some immediate and some much later development in the area.

Of the two pieces of Common Land north of the Riding Gate Brook, the larger piece No 8C of 13 perches up to Brook Bottom land was awarded to Robert Haslam who simply added it to his nearest field called Thomasson Meadow. The smaller piece No 44B of one perch area was awarded to Nathaniel Haslam who proceeded to build the cottage now No 75 called 'Ferndale'.

Robert Haslam who took over Top o'th' Knotts (West) Farm on his father John's death in 1784, died himself on 17th May 1809 and amongst his bequests he left to his stepson John Hamer those cottages in the occupation of Richard Manchester, John Haslam, ??? Entwistle, Ann Grundy and Richard Scowcroft. We think this is the group of cottages just over the bridge into Riding Gate now including Nos 59, 61, 63 & 65. This bequest completed the breakdown of all the Riding Gate cottages away from the Top o'th' Knotts (West) estate, apart from the Lower Knotts cottages and those adjacent to Top o'th' Knotts Farm.

Figure 24 Old Green Cottages - 1940.

Chapter VI   RIDING GATE AREA   1800-1900

The Enclosure Act of 1797 was the catalyst for development in the Riding Gate area and, as can be seen from the Enclosure Award Plan, all the freeholders of the old Riding Gate properties were allotted Awards in the immediate area, alongside either Riding Gate Lane or Tottington Road.

Nathaniel Haslam had two pieces Nos 44A and 44B. On the latter, being a small area just north of the brook in the original Riding Gate area, was built a cottage No 75. The allotment of 44A was left undeveloped for some years, as was the whole eastern side of the lane apart from the two allotments fronting on to both the lane and Tottington Road. These were Awards No 42 to Ralph Entwistle and No 41 to Thomas Haslam.

Thomas Haslam had built the pair of cottages Nos 227/229 Tottington Road by the time of his death in 1812, in one of which lived his son John. Thomas bequeathed to his son John these two cottages and the whole of No 41 Allotment as well as *'All the stone now got, being on the road-side adjoining for the purpose of building thereon'*. John Haslam proceeded to build two more cottages on the corner (now a single house No 211) with the datestone of 1816 carrying his name John Haslam and Margaret his wife. At this time this area was referred to as the 'Nook'.

Margaret Haslam was the eldest daughter of James Horrocks of Hill End Farm who lived to be over 100 years of age. This was a remarkable age to achieve in this period but all the more remarkable as his father lived in the time of Oliver Cromwell. His father William was born in 1657 and after his first wife had died he remained a widower for many years until in 1741 he married his 28 year old housekeeper when he was 84 years old. Young James Horrocks was born March 26th, 1744.

James Horrocks lived at Hill End Farm, Harwood and was noted as living there in the 1841 Census. During the next two years he went to live with his eldest daughter Margaret Haslam of the Nook. The Chambers Journal of October 21st, 1847 reporting on his great age and extraordinary background notes that James' son-in-law John Haslam, then aged 62, was *'harder of hearing than himself'*.

James Horrocks died on September 14th, 1844 at the Nook, Harwood aged 100 years, 5 months and 6 days and was buried in the graveyard of St Maxentius. His gravestone can be seen adjacent to the old Chapel Tower.

John Haslam died 19th February 1855 leaving his estate to his children Martha (Holt), Jane, William, James and Margaret.

Figure 25 William Horrocks aged 86 in 1743

Figure 26 Elizabeth Horrocks his second wife aged 28 in 1743

Figure 27 James Horrocks: aged 100 years in 1844. (C A Duval)

The Enclosure Award No 42 to Ralph Entwistle of Old Green had a frontage on both Riding Gate Lane and Tottington Road and on the latter was built the 'Britannia' public house in about 1812 with a bowling green to the rear. The earliest record of the publican was Mr. Andrew Hamer in 1832 who was also noted at the Britannia in the 1841 Census with his wife Margaret, five sons and four daughters. By 1853 Robert Bullough was the publican and in 1871, Thomas Ramsden. The Harwood Township Vestry Meetings were held at the Britannia until 1873, when the teetotal members voted to move the meetings to the new Walsh's Institute. The Scowcroft Diaries also note that Andrew Hamer formerly of the Britannia Inn died in 1873 aged 78 years.

Sometime in the 1880s it ceased to be a public house and in 1892 the GPO Directory notes Mr. G W Nelson, a paper-maker living at Britannia House, 231 Tottington Road and the house has continued as a private residence ever since. On June 2nd, 1900, the Scowcroft Diaries note that George Nelson of Britannia House fell out of his back bedroom window and was killed. The Inquest returned a verdict of Accidental Death.

Looking at the western side of Riding Gate Lane starting at the Green, a name which was initially given to the area between the Riding Gate Brook and the Tottington Road junction, it seemed quite natural when new buildings were erected to call the old established property of the Entwistles 'Old Green'. The strip of land between Old Green and the brook had been part of the Entwistle family property and in the early 1800s a terrace of cottages was built with an access road between Old Green and the new cottage fronts. In the 1841 Census thirteen families were noted as living in this enlarged Old Green group. The first two have basement cellars possibly built for loomshops.

Down the lane to Brook Bottom Farm, the Top o'th' Brow cottages on the left housed seven families in 1841. Additional cottages had been built since the Enclosures of 1797 when there were only two, 19 and 21 were probably the original pair and would be the two dwelling houses mentioned in Thomas Haslam's Will of 7th January 1808 and bequeathed to his son John. At this time they were occupied by William Collier and Michael Haworth (the freeholder in 1797). In 1855, on John Haslam's death, these two cottages were left to his trustees and were then occupied by Robert Heyes and William Hamer.

Coming back from the junction of Brookbottom Lane with Riding Gate Lane, within Allotment No 40B awarded to John Brooks was built a terrace of six cottages at right angles to the lane with an additional one at the end being parallel to the lane. It was logical to call this new development on the Green, 'New Green'. The first recorded indenture of sale is dated 9th December 1837 and it is likely that they were built in the early 1800s with loom-shop cellars/basements. The end property on Riding Gate Lane has been a shop and bakery and tradition suggests it has also been a beer-house, although no evidence can be found.

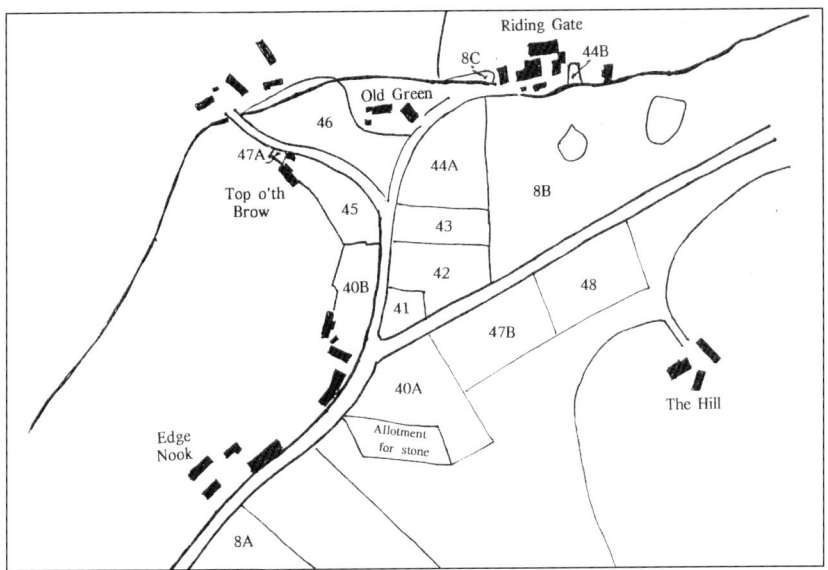

Award No	Owner	Area	Property eventually built
8A	Robert Haslam	4.3.39	Grey Mare Cottages
8B	Robert Haslam	8.1.34	Raikes Farm
8C	Robert Haslam	0.0. 1	
40A	John Brooks	1.1. 1	Tottington Rd Cottages
40B	John Brooks	0.1.27	New Green
41	Thomas Haslam	0.0.38	The Nook and Cottages
42	Ralph Entwistle	0.2.30	Britannia Inn etc.
43	James Entwistle	0.1.31	New Green Terrace
44A	Nathaniel Haslam	1.0. 4	Rose Bank etc.
44B	Nathaniel Haslam	0.0. 1	Ferndale
45	Oliver Ormrod	0.1.35	Riding Gate Mews
46	Henry Isherwood	1.0.19	Mission & High Meadow
47A	Michael Howarth	0.0. 5	
47B	Michael Howarth	1.0.23	
48	Devisees John Haslam	1.0.10	Knowles Buildings & Hill Brow

Figure 28 Enclosure Awards in Riding Gate, 1801 and subsequent developments.

Figure 29 Cottages and beerhouse that became the 'Grey Mare' c1900.

Figure 30 Tottington Road c1930 with the 'Grey Mare' on right, Ox Shutt Gate Farm to left and Edge Nook centre.

Figure 31 Edge Nook on Tottington Road c.1905: rebuilding of the road by TUDC.

Figure 32 Riding Gate junction with Tottington Road showing the Nook Cottages and the old Britannia Inn at top c1910.

Figure 33 Top o'th' Brow: on the field side or 'front': the open doorway is a passage to the rear - c1970.

Figure 34 New Green in 1961: built as a terrace of hand loom weavers cottages.

Figure 35 Riding Gate: entrance over the bridge on to the north side of the brook to the original 'Riding Gate' - c1910.

Figure 36 Riding Gate Cottage c1937: reputed to be one of the early non-conformists' meeting houses.

Figure 37 Riding Gate cottages: known as the 'City' with 'Ferndale' on the right and Top o'th' Greaves at the rear - 1975.

Figure 38 Riding Gate Mission: built by Thomas Hardcastle in 1897.

In 1837 the New Green cottages were purchased by James Bolton at which time there were nine dwelling houses. James Bolton died in November 1876 and the trustees of his Will sold the property to Samuel Hamer described as a Provision Dealer of Harwood.

Later developments on Riding Gate Lane include Rose Bank or No 36 Riding Gate and New Green Terrace or Nos 26 and 28.

Rose Bank was built in c1850 on the Enclosure Award allotted to Nathaniel Haslam, and comprised of a detached cottage with just over two acres of land run as a small holding in 1851 by Thomas Haslam with his wife Alice and their two daughters Betty (20) and Ellen (12) and two year old son Thomas. The 1861 Census notes Betty Knowles, a widow and retired farmer living at Rose Bank with her unmarried son James (25). By 1871 Rose Bank is the home of Peter Knowles and family and in 1881 the home of Thomas Bolton (65) the stone merchant and his wife Martha (62). Thomas Bolton is noted as employing 40 men whilst his son Job (19) is working as a bookkeeper in a stone quarry. Thomas Bolton had lived in the Knowles Buildings in 1871, at that time employing three hands in his stone merchants business. It is thought that Thomas Bolton operated the quarry off Tottington Road adjacent to the Methodist Chapel, originating from the Enclosure Stone Quarry, but then much extended towards Hill Farm.

New Green Terrace (Nos 26/28) carries a datestone indicating its build in 1882 by James Green Knowles and his wife Alice. He was a grocer and tea dealer and had lived with his family at New Green in 1871 & 1881 and moved across the lane to his newly built house in 1882. James had previously lived with his widowed mother Betty Knowles at Rose Bank in 1861.

Another development in the Riding Gate area before the end of the century was the building of the Riding Gate Mission. In 1890, Rev R K Judson, Vicar of St Maxentius Church was keen to extend the Church Mission work into the outer areas of Bradshaw Parish which included the Riding Gate area of Harwood. The Rigby Mission was the first to be established in 1894 when Thomas Hardcastle converted part of the Rigby's Bleach Works building for use as a Mission. Thomas Hardcastle followed this with the building of Higher Bradshaw Mission opposite Brook Buildings on Bradshaw Road later in 1894 and lastly the Riding Gate Mission opening on October 4th, 1897. The last two Mission buildings were of corrugated iron sheeting construction with lined walls. The land for all three Mission buildings was given by Mr. J B Isherwood, the Lord of the Manor of Bradshaw. The Riding Gate Mission was built on Enclosure Award No 46 allotted to Mr. J B Isherwood's grandfather Henry.

Initially all three Missions were administered by the Vicar but after the Rev Judson's differences with Thomas Hardcastle, Mr. Hardcastle as Founder and President arranged a Trust Deed with the Manchester City Mission being appointed Trustees.

Regarding the allotments along the southwest side of Tottington Road awarded to Riding Gate freeholders, Allotment No 40A, awarded to John Brooks, was largely used for the commercial extension of the old Enclosure Stone Quarry. A pair of cottages were built onto the road c1820 that included likely loomshop basements.

Allotment No 47B awarded to Michael Haworth was not developed and remains open today, now owned jointly by the householders opposite to secure their open aspect across the road.

Allotment No 48 was initially awarded to the trustees of John Haslam; however, by 1816 this piece of land of just over one acre was divided into three parts as shown on the Hill Farm Estate Plan of that date.

The lower portion belonged to John Knowles, who had purchased the land and buildings on 25th June 1808 from Nathaniel Haslam, as indicated in the deeds of No 250. This along with its neighbours Nos 246 and 248 were probably all built together prior to 1808, each initially comprising a pair of back-to-back cottages, subsequently modified to three single dwellings. The cellars of the cottages were constructed on a through basis with half windows to the north - ideal for use as loomshops.

Soon afterwards a cottage was built a little lower down on the same piece of land but at right angles to Tottington Road. Two others were added by the 1880s, being numbers 240, 242 and 244. All these cottages, known collectively as Knowles Buildings, remained with the Knowles family and belonged to Peter Knowles through to the 1900s.

The middle portion of the allotment, No 48, was owned in 1816 by John Haslam, the owner of the Nook across the road, which had his named datestone. This road incline is referred to as Hill Brow on a map of the 1860s, but the pair of cottages built on this middle section was called Hill Nook. John Haslam died on the 19th September 1855 and left *'Two dwelling houses at Hill Nook in the occupation of Betty Smethurst and John Whittle'* to his daughter Margaret. James Scowcroft later owned them in 1890.

The 1816 plan shows the top section of Allotment No 48 owned by George Heaton. In the Will of Robert Haslam of Top o'th' Knotts of 17th May, 1809 he left

Figure 39 The former Britannia Inn built c1812.

Figure 40 Knowles Buildings: built c1808 as cottages with loom shops in basement cellars, Hill Nook Cottage is on the left.

Figure 41 Hill Brow Cottages built by George Heaton c1809.

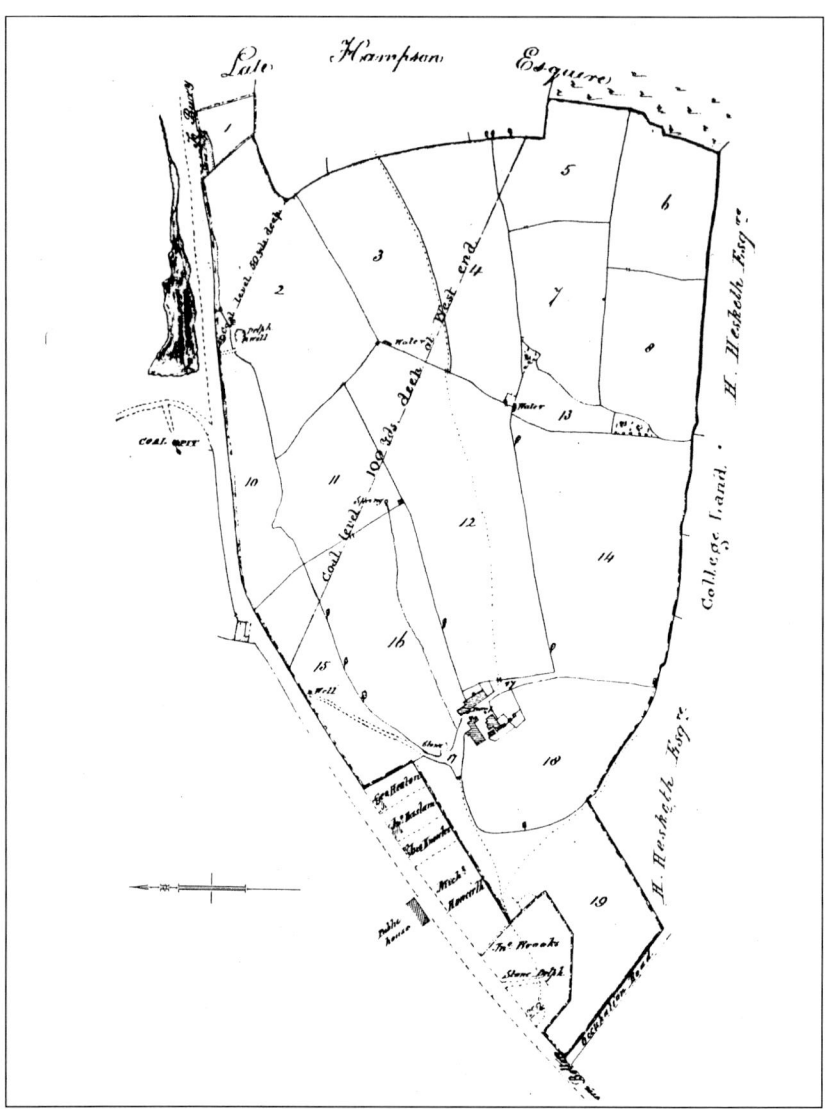

Figure 42 Plan of the Hill Estate, Harwood, in 1816, showing the land ownership on Tottington Road. The chapel has not yet been built and just above its future site is the old Enclosure Act quarry of John Brooks. The Britannia Inn is built and the sites of John Knowles, James Haslam and George Heaton had already been built up with 'Knowles', 'Hill Nook' and Hill Brow cottages. Raikes Farm is marked while the reservoir and associated coal pit are in existence. Two coal levels are marked as draining towards Riding Gate.

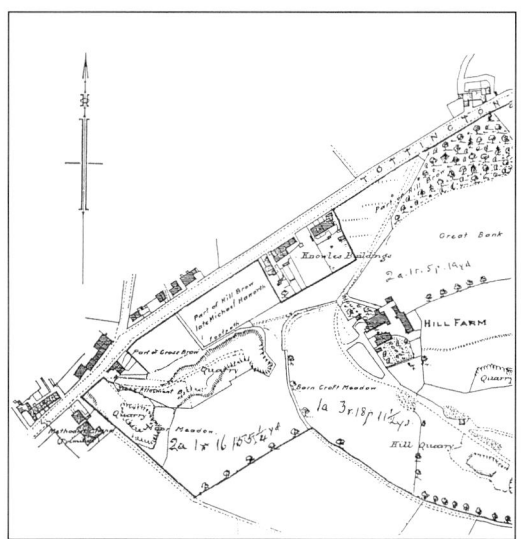

Figure 43 Part of Hill Farm plan, c 1890, showing the lower Tottington Road area. The old 1841 chapel is shown with the new 1890 buildings to its rear. The quarry is by now much extended towards Hill Farm. Properties now numbered 227/9, originally said to have been a bakehouse and shop, have been built below the Britannia Inn.

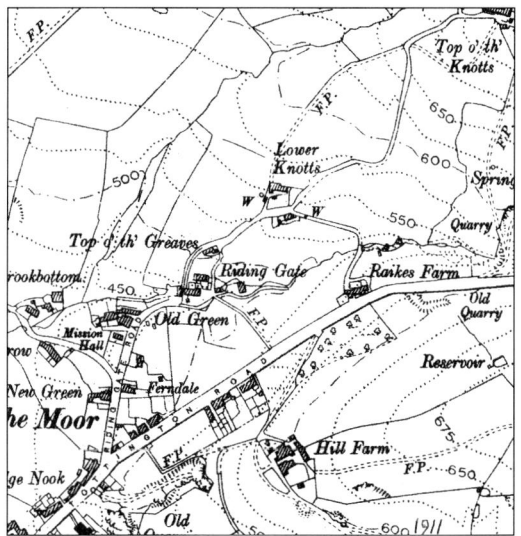

Figure 44 OS map of 1911 showing Riding Gate and Tottington Road, the area remained largely unchanged until after World War II.

to his daughter Rachel Heaton (wife of George Heaton) *'a piece of land now in possession of George Heaton called Hill Nook'*, suggesting that the cottages had not then been built. The 1850 OS Map shows the terrace of three cottages while the fourth across the end at right angles to the road is later shown on the 1893 OS Map.

The three original cottages 260, 262 and 264 were offered for sale by auction in July 1832 at the same time as Raikes Farm, the two lots being jointly owned by eight parties, presumably various members of the Haslam and Heaton families. At this time the cottages were occupied by Robert Horrocks, Thomas Bolton and Phillip Vickers with Robert Ramwell occupying the adjacent land along with Raikes Farm across the road. In 1898 James Heaton owned these cottages.

The last allotments originating from freeholders of Knotts/Riding Gate are those of Robert Haslam of Top o'th' Knotts Nos 8A and 8B.

Allotment 8A is the piece of land immediately below the Primitive Methodist Chapel built in 1841 noted on the 1850 OS Map as the Hephzibah Chapel. It is said that this chapel had its early roots in local cottages, including No 67 Riding Gate, where meetings were held.

In the northern corner of this allotment No 8A were built a pair of cottages noted on the 1850 OS Map as Side o'th' Moor. It seems one of the cottages operated as a beer-house which eventually developed into the Grey Mare Inn, although this was not marked as a public house on the local maps until 1939, However, the 1841 Census includes a William Smith of Side o'th' Moor described as a Publican, but the first real evidence is shown in the 1881 Census when James Hill is noted as Beer Seller at Side o'th' Moor Grey Mare Beer House.

Allotment No 8B was the largest land award to Robert Haslam on which he established an *'independent farm holding'*. On his death in 1809 he left to his son James *'All those new erected buildings now in possession of Abraham Settle on Hogscar and the Raikes'*. If James should die without lawful issue then the estate and buildings should go to his sisters Elizabeth, Mary and Rachel (Heaton). It may have been James Haslam's early demise that led to the multi-ownership selling on at the Auction Sale on 25th July 1832 at the Britannia Inn to the next owner, James Heaton.

Hogscar was the name given to the strip of land between Riding Gate Brook and Tottington Road from Riding Gate up to the western boundary of Robert Haslam's land. Raikes is a well used term for a steep sided valley and Riding Gate Brook at Riding Gate enters a long length of ravines or 'raikes'. The Enclosure Map notes our Tottington Road as Boason's Hill Highway, Boason's

Hill being the highest point of the ridge at High Barn Farm. In the middle of the 1800s this road was often called Raikes Lane until finally Tottington Road was established in the 1890s. A similar variation in name happened with this holding, initially called Hogscar, it was confirmed Raikes Farm in the 1890s.

In order for James Hardcastle to mine under Raikes Farm land an Indenture of 26th January, 1849 with James Heaton allowed access to 'a mine of coal called Bradshaw or Harwood Mine' in and under Raikes Farm land. James Heaton died in 1854 and left Raikes Farm to his son Robert Heaton.

In 1887 the then owner of Raikes Farm, William Haslam Heaton, sold the property to Peter Ormrod who died two years later in 1889 and the Trustees of his Will sold the farm to Jethro Haslam in the early 1900s.

In 1872, the Bolton statutory area for the supply and/or testing of water was extended to include Bradshaw and Harwood and in 1880 a survey was made of the whereabouts and quality of the water used by the Riding Gate population. These were described as follows:

No 22 PUMP AT TANNERS FARM. (the name at this time of Oxshutt Gate Farm) *This is a pump in a closed well in Mr. Hopwood's farmyard and affords a supply for five houses.* (Edge Nook) *The quality of the water is considered fairly good, but is not always equal.*

No 23 SIDE OF THE MOOR WELL. This is a well sunk in rock at the corner of the houses which are supplied from it. (Grey Mare Cottages) *It is a little below the ground level and uncovered. The supply is not continuous and is often empty in dry weather. Sewer water passes on the surface near the well and may occasionally get into it, otherwise the water is considered to be good.*

No 24 HEPHZIBAH WELL. Supplying eight houses. (cottages opposite chapel on Tottington Road) *It is a stone cistern about eight feet below ground level with nine steps, down which wet weather washings run. The well is often dry and dirty. When tested, the water appeared to be good*

No 25 EDGE NOOK WELL. A stone built well on the roadside reached by eight steps. Has flag cover with earth over. Water fed by iron pipe, probably from the rock quarried near to (across the road). *It is very often dry and in rain times is muddy. It serves about 27 houses and when visited appeared to be of good quality.* (Note: this well would be used by Edge Nook and Nook Cottages and possibly New Green)

No 26 BROOK BOTTOM PIPE. This supplies 21 houses by means of an iron pipe fixed in wall forming side of the brook and the roadway. The source is not known, but the supply is abundant at all times; the quality is considered good. (Note: will supply Top o'th' Brow and Old Green Cottages)

NO 27 TUNNEL MOUTH AT RIDING GATE. About 20 houses are supplied from an iron pipe fixed in the wall by the brook side and communicating with an old coal pit tunnel. A good stream issues and is never dry. Quality considered very good. An accumulation of ashes above the bank should be moved. (Note: in the northern side of the brook adjacent Nos 59 and 61 and used by all Riding Gate Cottages)

No28 RIDING GATE WELL. This is a well used by many of the people who also use the Tunnel Mouth Pipe No 27. It is by the brook side having the same level as the brook. It is stone built and partially covered with flags. It is never dry, but not always clear. (Note: sited in the southerly bank opposite No 75)

No 29 HILL BROW SPOUT. Some 11 houses are served from a spout fixed in the wall at the roadside, the water being brought from a reservoir on the hillside by means of an open channel through a field, where it may be polluted. The quality is doubtful. Most of the tenants use it for washing purposes only and go for food water to Edge Nook Well No 25 800 yards distance. (Note: served Hill Brow and Knowles Cottages)

No 30 LOWER KNOTTS WELL This is an uncovered stone built well at the front of a roadside fence and the washings from the road can run in as also from gardens on higher ground behind the wall. The sewage from the houses runs into the gardens through an open channel to within 10 yards of the Well. Seven Houses are supplied with this water which fails in dry weather. (Note: would supply all Lower Knotts and Greaves Cottages)

The farms of Old Neds, Hoyles Fold and Top o'th' Knotts had their own wells and/or supply reservoirs.

All the toilets would be earth-closets, the sewage from which would be spread over the local fields. In the late 1800s the closets were cleaned out by 'night soil' workers collecting by horse and cart to be spread on open fields.

With the change in occupation patterns, particularly the loss of hand loom weaving and coal mining jobs, and the movement of local factory/mill workers to the newer 'estates' of Lee Gate and Bradshaw Brow, the Riding Gate area became a little run down. By 1891 there were thirteen unoccupied houses in the Riding Gate area while the Top o'th' Knotts and Swine Trough Cottages were also empty; the latter were never occupied again and became ruins.

Chapter VII   INDUSTRIAL ACTIVITIES OF THE AREA

Harwood was largely an agricultural economy up to the middle 1700s, supplemented by fringe activities such as handloom weaving, coal mining, and quarrying. These supplementary and part-time occupations developed into full time jobs as the demand for their output grew and the work became better organised.

HANDLOOM WEAVING

This domestic form of weaving came about as a requirement of self-sufficiency when the agricultural society required clothing and bedding. Only the well to do could afford to have these made for them, while the majority of the population had to make their own. Most local farmers kept sheep and the wool output could readily be spun into yarn which could then be woven. This activity started as a domestic necessity but, over the 18th century, developed into a type of domestic industry when handlooms enabling a fairly wide piece of cloth to be woven were introduced and operated by skilled specialist workers. The lengths of woollen cloth were cleaned and fulled at the Manor Fulling Mill.

By the mid-1700s, the general demand grew for finer cloth rather than the coarser woollens and the changeover to cotton began. The raw material sources now being out of the weaver's control meant that the supply of cotton, either raw or in spun yarn, could only be obtained from merchants, or as called in the Bolton area, chapmen.

These chapmen became an important factor in the local handloom weaving industry, who not only supplied cotton yarn but also bought the lengths of cotton cloth. The same merchants arranged for the necessary bleaching and dyeing before selling on at the markets in Bolton, Manchester, or indeed London. These merchants beginning in one local area invariably grew to have offices and warehouses in both Manchester and London. Some also rented out handlooms for the weavers to work in their own dwellings.

As the local highways were unsuitable for long distance cart traffic, the same chapmen organised packhorse trains by which raw materials and finished goods were transported. These consisted of ten, twenty or more ponies and apart from servicing the weaving trade, were the local carriers for all manner of goods.

Although handloom weaving in the simplest form was a loom set up by a cottager in his back kitchen on which he worked in the slack times from his normal agricultural work, by the late 1700s this form had been overtaken by a more commercial full time occupation. This change encouraged special 'loom-shops' to be established which were generally in 'half-cellars'. These basements or ground floor rooms were usually in the earth up to window height, and had earth or flag floors . This gave a dampish environment which helped to maintain a good yarn strength, particularly desirable for the weft.

Probably the oldest loom-shop remaining in the area is at Top o'th' Knotts (West) Farm adjacent to the farmhouse and still called the 'loomhouse'. This building is of a small cottage form and that may well have been its origin. Another example of an early adaptation of an existing building is referred to in an Old Green document as the 'loomshop'.

The Riding Gate area has a number of specialist loom-shops built within dwelling houses, the earliest being built in 1795 by George Heaton and his wife Rachel at Lower Knotts. Although the front of the pair of houses is of the period style, the rear downstairs has a long window of sixteen mullioned window lights running across the rear of both dwellings. The earth runs up to the bottom of the windows and the combination of the two features, the earthy dampness and plenty of north light gives an ideal environment for weaving.

A similar early example was on the extension to No 79 Riding Gate which was bequeathed to Thomas Haslam by his father, John Haslam who died in 1784, given with *'liberty to build on a further bay building'*. This early extension was discovered on the renovation of No 77 in the 1980s which revealed the previous gable end of the extension facing the brook having a row of eight mullioned window lights, which was probably built as a loom-shop. Other likely loom-shops are the half-cellars of Nos 59 and 61 Riding Gate which have connecting cellars, each with a small row of mullioned lights on to the old Top o'th' Knotts occupation road to the rear.

Another sign of previous commercial activity remains in Nos 69 and 71 where the downstairs rear room on No 69 protrudes behind a front room of No 71. Similarly this can be seen at Lower Knotts where a rear room of No 85 protrudes into No 83. This form of layout under previous common ownership was established for a special use before a later split into separate dwellings.

Later post enclosure examples of half-cellar loom-shops are evident in the Knowles Buildings, Nos 246, 248 and 250 Tottington Road where half windows of the cellars can be seen at pavement level from which steps lead up to the ground floor of each dwelling. Similarly at New Green where there were once five separate cottages in the terrace at right angles to the road, each had half-cellars constructed as loom-shops. Although by the time of the 1841 Census handloom weaving was beginning to decline, there were a number of weavers noted in the Riding Gate area.

Figure 45 Top o'th'Knotts Loom House: probably an old worker's cottage used by hand loom weavers - 2002.

Figure 46 The Lower Knotts loom shop purpose built by George Heaton in 1795 as it appeared in 2002.

Figure 47 Nos 77 & 79 Riding Gate: photographed from behind Ferndale - 1980.

Figure 48 The long row of lights indicating a loom shop, discovered during renovation of No 79 - 1980.

Unfortunately, at this time there was no differentiation made between handloom and powerloom weavers so we cannot be sure that all the following weavers worked on handlooms. At Top o'th' Knotts were James Platt and Joseph Nuttall; at Lower Knotts were Robert, Mary and Matty Heaton and Thomas Entwistle. Weavers noted in Riding Gate included Henry Fielding, Joseph Ramsden, William Horrocks, John Dootson, John and Richard Greenhalgh, John Thomasson Senior and Junior. Old Green had James, Alice, John and Peggy Hamer, Samuel Horrocks, Samuel Bromiley and John Howarth - some of these may have lived in the cottages along Riding Gate Brook, Nos 51, 53, 55 and 57 Riding Gate. New Green had Joseph and Ann Howarth and Robert and Esther Walsh. In the Knowles Building dwellings were weavers named Edward Whittle, Abraham Hardman, John Boardman, Hannah Heaton, Sarah Platt and Jane Entwistle.

In 1851, handloom weavers were described specifically and those noted included James Platt and Mary Rothwell at Top o'th' Knotts cottages, as was Robert Heaton at Lower Knotts and John and Betty Ramsden at Old Green.

In 1861 there were fewer handloom weavers noted with Mary Heaton at Lower Knotts; trade must have been very bad as husband Robert Heaton was then working as a road labourer. Joseph Ramsden is still noted as a handloom weaver at Riding Gate.

By 1871 the only handloom weaver still working in the Riding Gate area was Joseph Ramsden, then aged seventy years.

The decline of the handloom weaving trade was caused by the dramatic increase in lower cost powerloom weaving and many local handloom weavers took up employment in the various local textile mills. Although Bolton mills generally specialised in spinning we did have some local weaving factories within walking distance for Harwood folk. These included the New Eagley Mills of the Ashworths near the Oaks, Walker's Spring Vale Mill at Edgworth, Bottoms and Ferns Mills and several others in Tottington and Walshaw. Many other handloom weavers also left their old trade to take up employment in the local bleachworks of Two Brooks, Bradshaw Hall, Firwood, Horrobin and Harwood Vale.

COAL MINING

We have had coal mining in our area for a very long time, probably starting with the digging from outcrops by the Romans on the Affetside ridge. This developed into shallow and deep shaft working which continued until the late 1800s. The getting of coal for domestic use was undertaken by the local farm workers on a seasonal basis, that is in the slack times of farming. By the mid-1700s the developing mining activity was contracted out to the professional operators. who would pay a tonnage rent to the landowner holding the coal mining rights. These operators would employ full time colliers.

The earliest reference to coal mining in the Knotts area was in 1620 when Henry Haworth, the then owner of the two Top o'th' Knotts farms gave permission to his stepson Robert Haslam *'to get coal from the coal pit'*. Robert could also sink other coal pits throughout the two farms. The existing coal pit would probably be on the north side of their land in Coal Pit Field bordering with Bradshaw land at Affetside. This family arrangement was conditional on Robert Haslam supplying his stepfather Henry Haworth with coal for his *'necessary firing and fuel'*, signifying that the pit was supplying coal for domestic use only. By 1670, the ownership of the Knotts farms was such that Top o'th' Knotts (West) belonged to the Haslam family while the other two farms of Top o'th' Knotts (East) and Hoyles Fold were owned by the Lever family.

The first record we have of coalmining in the Lever farms of Knotts was a shaft sinking contract dated 27th November 1738 when Samuel Lever engaged Edmund Lomas of Tottington and James Holt of Bradshaw to sink a rectangular shaft of 6ft.4ins by 4ft.6ins down to coal (approximately 100ft depth) and to drive a water drainage sough to the 'Old Pit' at the top of Fell Meadow, one of the northerly fields of Top o'th' Knotts (East) farm. The contract price was fifteen shillings per yard depth of the shaft and one shilling and eight pence per yard for the water drainage sough. The sinking was to be completed within ten months and the sinkers were expected to draw any water out of the shaft and allow the owners any coal mined. Samuel Lever was to supply the boring rods but the contractors were *'at the expense of sharpening and mending the same as often as occasion shall require'*. Reference to the connecting drainage tunnel with the old pit confirms coal mining on the Lever land from at least 1700 and probably from their purchase of the farms in 1669.

Coal mining was continued by a mine operator working on behalf of the Lever family in their northern fields of Top o'th' Knotts (East) and in 1765 suffered some trespass from coal miners working on the Bradshaw land adjacent to Affetside. Thomas Lever, the then owner of Top o'th' Knotts (East) claimed that his coal pit had suffered trespass from James Haddock and Joshua Haslam of Tottington who were operating the Higher Coal Pit in Bradshaw belonging to Nathaniel Isherwood Esq. of Marple, the Lord of the Manor of Bradshaw. The agreement dated 27th February 1765 bound the parties on a £500 fine to accept arbitration on the complaint - we do not know the result of the arbitration. Another existing record regarding coal pits on the Lever farms was about a court case of March 1828 when Abraham Leach, the tenant of Hoyles Fold, claimed damages for the loss of a cow falling down the unfenced shaft of Ladder Pit operated by Mr. Scowcroft.

Evidence of another coal pit in the Lever family estate is shown on a map of Hill Farm dated 1816. On the north side of Tottington Road near the entrance to the old stone quarry was a reservoir fed by Riding Gate Brook. This lodge in turn appears to have fed a water wheel used for winding and/or pumping from another coal pit shaft just on the north bank of Riding Gate Brook. This was working in 1816 and on an 1844 map is designated *'Old Wheel Pit'*. This reservoir embankment was broken down in the 1960s when the adjacent quarry was extended.

Since the early record in 1620 of the coal pit on Top o'th' Knotts (West) Farm there was continuing mining activity operated by the owner. However, when Robert Haslam took over the farm in 1784 on his father John's death it appears that he did not wish to continue coal mining on his own account and formed an agreement dated 6th August 1791 with his brother Thomas Haslam that Thomas should manage the coal mining on the property in return for one third part of the profit made on coal mined. Thomas Haslam was at this time tenant of Old Ned's Farm and was probably operating his own pit on Old Neds land - this pit was working in 1797 as noted in the Enclosure Award details.

When Robert Haslam died on 17th May, 1809, this agreement of 1791 was confirmed and the other two thirds of the coal rights were divided equally between Robert's daughters, Elizabeth Haslam, Mary Hamer, Rachel Heaton and his grand-children Ralph and Betty Fletcher, the children of his daughter Alice, deceased. Brother Thomas had also to pay to the above £10 yearly for his third share. Thomas Haslam died in 1812 leaving all his Knotts' mining interests to his son John.

This partnership had both rights and responsibilities. They and/or their agents and workmen had power to sink any pits or drive tunnels on the Top o'th' Knotts (West) Estate for the purpose of getting coal. They could make roads to the pits for carriage of coal and could get stone for making these roads as well as for any necessary building or engine house. The shareholders were responsible for all the expenses, paying the workmen's wages, providing all the wood for supporting the roof, ropes, wheels, engines and maintaining the same. The roads to the pits had to be maintained and the shafts filled in as and when the pits were exhausted. Any new partners were to be approved by all the shareholders. Proper books of account were to be kept concerning coal got and sold and the dividends were paid quarterly. The shareholders had to pay Robert Haslam, the new owner of Top o'th' Knotts (West) Farm, one shilling per week for as long as coal was worked from his land.

The oldest mine workings plan we can find is dated 1848/51 which details the extensive workings, mainly on the south side of Riding Gate Brook. It also shows several old coal pit shaft sites on the north side of the brook which had serviced coaling operations up to 1848. They were marked as *'Old Works'*. One shaft marked as a Ladder Pit was on the northwest corner of the lane running from Raikes Farm to Lower Knotts. There were also coal pit shaft sites adjacent to No 91 Lower Knotts alongside the old occupation road to Top o'th' Knotts as was a second shaft just northwest of Top o'th' Greaves.

Another coal pit site is marked some 100yds northwest of No 83 Lower Knotts in the Lower Lime Field which is called 'Ringing Pit'. A tunnel is marked, running southwesterly from the Ringing Pit to Riding Gate Brook adjacent to No 59 Riding Gate, which was probably a drainage sough but could also have been a drift entry to the workings. The remains of the outlet tunnel can be seen in the stream bank.

A small plan of 1838 shows details of a tunnel between Brookbottom and Riding Gate, probably connected with the use of a water wheel at Riding Gate Pit. This could have been for winding coal or pumping water from the lower levels. Riding Gate Pit shaft was uncovered by Mr. Ernest Parton in 1979 in his garden at 59 Riding Gate being 8ft square and 135ft deep.

Water encroachment into the coal workings was an ever present problem and the Bradshaw Colliery pits had arranged all their levels to drain into an underground reservoir at the most southerly pit. A beam engine pumped up water from this 156 feet deep shaft to an outlet tunnel 48 feet from the surface through which it drained naturally into Bradshaw Brook. This same pumping pit was later utilised by James Hardcastle's Harwood Colliery when a drainage sough from the New Pit workings under Castle Farm was run down to the pumping pit opposite Bradshaw Works entrance. This sough must have been nearly a mile long and was tunneled c1845 to make mining a practical proposition in the deeper levels on the southeast side of Riding Gate Brook. It would appear that on the northern side of Riding Gate Brook all the coal that could safely (i.e. dry) be worked was taken by 1845 with a minimum of pumping and only the tunneling of the drainage sough by James Hardcastle & Co enabled further coal to be mined.

Examination of the dates noted on the 1844/51 Plan indicated that the extensions of workings into the deeper parts of the seam started in 1847. The shaft depth of Riding Gate Pit on the north side of Riding Gate was 135 feet. This depth could have allowed for drainage water from an underground reservoir to be pumped up to the brook, although later it would have connected with the new drainage sough to Bradshaw Hall pumping pit.

The new Harwood Colliery was managed by James Hardcastle & Co to supply coal to Bradshaw Hall Bleachworks.

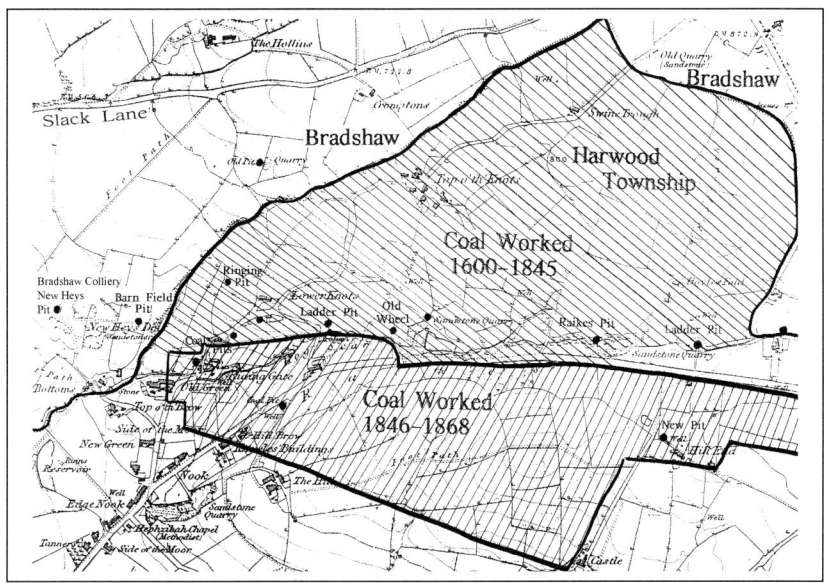

Figure 49 Map showing areas of Harwood mined 1600-1805 & 1846-1868, all the recorded shafts are marked.

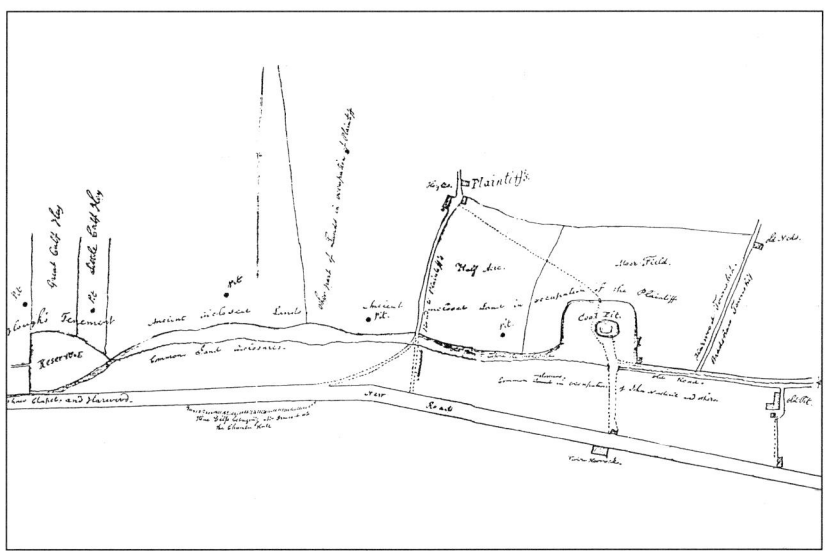

Figure 50 Plan showing the ladder pit near Hoyles Fold, the subject of a law suit by Hoyles' tenant Abraham Leach, who had lost a cow down '*Mr. Scowcroft's pit shaft*'.

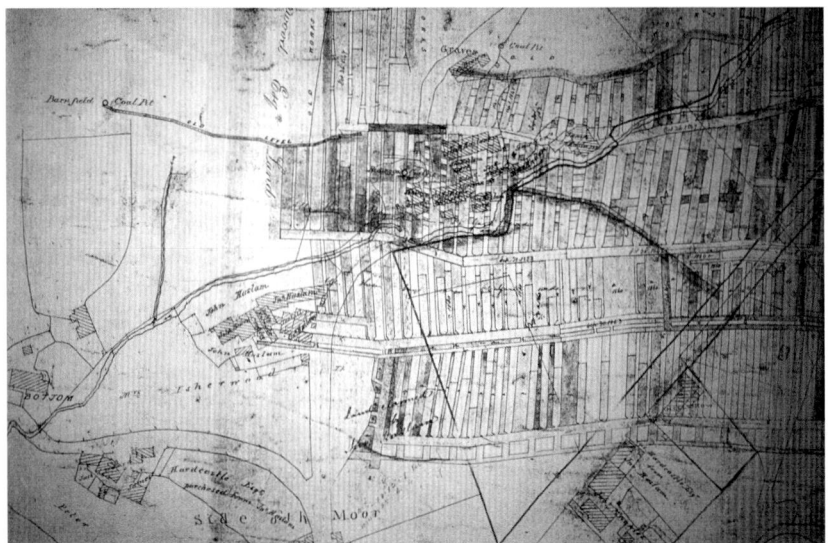

Figure 51 Underground workings at Harwood Colliery: coal was mined in panels of 15 ft wide leaving similar widths of pillars to support the roof, Tottington Road & Riding Gate can be seen superimposed on the plan - 1844.

Figure 52 Riding Gate shaft, adjacent to No 59 Riding Gate, prepared for 'capping' by the NCB. The shaft was 8 ft square, 135 ft deep and is marked centrally on the above plan - 1979.

They proceeded to buy/rent the local mining rights to allow the getting of this coal. These arrangements included rents etc to John and William Hall of Height Barn, the Hulme Trust for High Barn, Hill End Farm, James Hampson of Castle Farm, Peter Ormrod of Hill Farm, James Heaton of Raikes Farm and several freeholders of Riding Gate cottage properties including James Haslam, John Haslam, Edward Lomax and John Ormrod.

The first shafts used by James Hardcastle & Co were Riding Gate Pit and the Raikes shaft at the lane end of Hill Farm. These workings are dated from 1847 to 1860. The two later pit shafts were the Raikes Pit on the north western side of Tottington Road between the lane ends of Top o'th' Knotts and Hoyles Farms, dated 1859 and the New Pit adjacent to Hill End Farm also dated 1859.

The New Pit shaft was 114 yards down to the Lower Foot coal seam of 1ft 9ins to 2ft in thickness. The coal was mined on a pillar and stall method taking bays of fifteen feet of coal and leaving a similar width of pillar between traveling galleries about fifty yards apart. The seam dips southerly from Top o'th' Knotts down to the lower drainage level with an additional dip down towards Bradshaw. Coal was raised by steam engine at both Raikes and New Pit, being wound in small tubs holding 2 cwts each, slung two at a time onto the winding rope. The men rode down in the same tubs. Winding up men and coal continued all day with the steam engines used for pumping out drainage water as and when necessary.

The coal would be held on the pit bank to be taken away by horse and cart. Flags jutting out of the wall can still be seen alongside Tottington Road close to the old shaft at the bottom of Hill Farm lane adjacent to 268 Tottington Road. These would form the loading ramp under which the cart would reverse to be loaded from the pit bank above.

At this earlier Raikes Pit shaft there was a tragic accident on December 8th, 1847, soon after the pit opened. The winding rope became detached from the drum dropping seven colliers who were riding in two tubs, a distance of forty yards to the pit bottom. Three were killed and the other four were severely injured. The inquest was held at Andrew Hamer's Britannia Inn on Tottington Road before the coroner, Mr. T F Dearden. Amongst the jurors were James Chadwick, Samuel Scowcroft, John Kershaw, Samuel Kershaw, John Brookes, Thomas Morris, William Street and John Hamer, all farmers or tradesmen of Bradshaw. From Harwood were Charles Hopwood, farmer of Hardy Mill, Robert Haslam, farmer of Top o'th' Knotts (West), John Ormrod, farmer of Hill Farm, Robert Hamer, farmer of Nab Fold, John Scowcroft, farmer of Longsight Farm and William Bradshaw, schoolmaster at Longsight Wesleyans. One solicitor represented the mine owner James Hardcastle and another the relatives of the deceased. Robert Lomax of Lomax Fold (Harwood Lodge) was also present.

The colliers killed were William Smith (46), John Ramwell (15) and Wright Jackson (16). Those injured were James Ball (16), John Entwistle (18), William Spence (18) and Thomas Ball (13) - the latter the only one expected to recover.

The Inquest Report, although making rather sad reading, does elaborate on some aspects of the working of the pits. They started work underground at 6.00am and the miners went down the pit from 5.30am by riding two at a time in the two tubs slung on the winding ropes. A contributory factor to the tragedy was that rather than the four men riding there were seven at the time of the accident. There did not appear to be a mechanical method of signaling to the steam-engine driver, the only way was by shouting up the shaft. The engine tenter or winder at the time of the accident was James Howarth (19) of Breightmet who had started work at 7.00 o'clock the previous night.

The manager/bookkeeper was Robert Heaton (28) of Harwood who was in charge of all surface duties while John Ramwell (49) of Bradshaw Brow was the underlooker or underground manager. Mr. Joseph Jackson of Bolton acted as colliery surveyor. He was a land agent/surveyor in practice in Bolton and probably worked for James Hardcastle's other mines in the area.

John Davenport (36), a getter of coal and a witness to the accident, said he had helped to sink the new shaft about twelve months previously. The machinery must therefore have been recently set up and was reported to be in good working order. The main fault was established as the failure of the fastening or lashing of the winding rope to the drum unfortunately coinciding with the overload of seven men instead of the recommended four.

This extension southwards of coal mining in Harwood starting in 1847 had a fairly short life and after twenty-one years finally closed down in 1868 when the New Pit was reported to have flooded.

The 1841 Census notes many coal miners living in the Riding Gate area of Harwood with a high proportion of youngsters and included Robert, James (14) and Edward Ramsden (11), James Ramsden, George Collier (14) and James Lomas, all of Top o'th' Brow. John Ramsden from Side o'th' Moor. John Horrocks (9), John Collier, Simon Platt (15), Joseph Platt (12), and Andrew Platt of Knowles Buildings. From Riding Gate were Edward Platt, Robert and John Greenhalgh, Thomas Greenhalgh, James and John Haslam, Robert Ramwell, John (15), James (14) and Thomas Ramsden (12), John Stevenson, James Marsden and James Lomax (11). Samuel Haslam, William Collier, Croshaw and

Samuel Rothwell (15) and James Platt lived at Old Green. James (15) and Simon Holt (12) lived at Swinetrough Cottages while John Nuttall, a banksman, Ashton Rothwell, Thomas and William Nuttall lived in Top o'th' Knotts Cottages. Ralph Lomax and William Aspinall (15) lived at Lower Knotts.

Although by today's standards some of these lads were far too young to be working underground, they were not by the standards of the time. The Coal Mines Act of 1842 made it illegal to employ any females or boys aged under ten below ground after 1st March 1843, so that John Horrocks, the nine year old boy in 1841 would be 'legal' by the time of the adoption of the Act in 1843.

In 1871 after the closure of Harwood Colliery, there were naturally less coal miners noted in the Census but still included were James Hamer of Hoyles Fold, James Scholes of Top o'th' Knotts cottages, James Entwistle of Hill End and James and Edwin Scholes also of Top o'th' Knotts cottages.

By 1881 only a few coal miners were noted in the Census and included John Turner of Side o'th' Moor, John and William Hulme, Peter Turner and Thomas Holt of Knowles Buildings and Thomas Hamer of Old Green. Bradshaw and Harwood Collieries had closed and the nearest coal mines operating were Breightmet, Tonge Moor, and other Bolton districts.

STONE QUARRYING

Starting as another fringe supplementary occupation when all the farms and settlements had their own stone delphs, particularly in the higher parts of Harwood, stone would be got for their own domestic buildings and walling. Up to the Enclosure Act, those with Commons rights could get turves and coal from where they could be found and stone could also be got for their own domestic use.

Among the first large quarries in Harwood were those established through the Enclosure Act in 1797 when two areas were allocated of half an acre each for the quarrying of stone. One such allotment was on the southeast side of Tottington Road just below the Riding Gate Lane junction. The other was on the north side of the lane leading to Brookfold, this lane now known as Brookfold Lane was then more aptly named Stone Pit Road. The Act required the Commissioners to *'assign, set out and appoint so many convenient part or pieces of the Commons, not exceeding one statute acre in the whole, as they shall think proper, for the purpose of getting stone, gravel, sand and other materials for making the public roads and ways which are within the Township of Harwood'*. The Surveyor of Highways appointed by the Commissioners was given the authority to decide when sufficient materials had been quarried. The quarries could then be sold by the Overseers and Constable who could apply the monies received in *'Aid of the Poor Rates'*.

Of the two Enclosure quarries, the one on Brookfold Lane was soon abandoned and a larger one developed below Castle Farm and adjacent to Asmus Fold on Hulme Trust land. The other quarry just off Tottington Road developed into the largest quarry in Harwood at this time and was of some two acres by 1847. This was finally abandoned in the early 1900s and the area adjacent to Tottington Road cleared for use by Tottington Road Methodist Chapel

In the latter half of the 1800s the abandoned Enclosure quarry on Brookfold Lane was developed as the Hardy Mill Quarry of the Hopwoods and eventually ran from Brookfold Lane westwards to just below Hill Farm and almost meeting up with the other Enclosure quarry on Tottington Road.

There were two other stone quarries, as well as the smaller delphs, in the Raikes area of the Riding Gate Brook valley; one below Hoyles Fold and the other below Top o'th' Knotts (East) Farm, both working in the 1840s. The latter quarry continued working on an intermittent basis until in 1961 it was reopened to supply ballast stone for local motorway construction. After a fatal accident in 1976, quarrying ceased and its infill by tipping continued over the following ten years. The site has now been restored to the original contours as grazing land.

The occupation of quarrymen was noted in the 1841 Census under *'stonegetter'* and included Thomas Smith, James and Thomas Bolton of Side o'th' Moor, Robert Clough of Riding Gate, Thomas Aspinall and James Lomax of Old Green. There were also *'stone masons'* noted who included Samuel Openshaw of New Green, Thomas and Edward Whittle of Knowles Buildings, Adam and James Brooks of Riding Gate and George Openshaw of Lower Knotts. The occupation of stonemason would have been in dressing and sizing stones for building use rather than in quarrying or getting the stone.

By 1861, 'quarryman' was a noted occupation and included Thomas Lowe and John Smith of Top o'th' Knotts, Lommy Taylor and Davenport Hamer of Swinetrough Cottages and Thomas Smith of Riding Gate.

In 1881, the Thomas Bolton mentioned in 1841 as previously living at Side o'th' Moor now lived at Rose Bank and was noted as a Stone Merchant employing forty men, while his son worked as the bookkeeper in the stone quarry. The Boltons probably ran the quarry off Tottington Road adjacent to the Methodist Chapel.

Quarrying continues today at the Brookfold Quarry by James Booth & Co. They are no longer quarrying building stone but shale which is used in brick making. Final closure and infilling are scheduled to be completed in approximately twelve years time.

Figure 53 Originally one of the Enclosure stone quarries, worked up to 1900, here being reclaimed for sports use - c1910.

Figure 54 Tottington Road quarry in 1964, getting stone ballast for the new St Peters Way: work ceased in 1976 after a fatal accident.

Chapter VIII   KNOTTS / HOYLES FOLD   1900-2000

Widower Elijah Lonsdale tenanted Top o'th' Knotts (West) in 1900 with his daughter Mary Jane who on December 23rd, 1896 had married John Scowcroft, son of Robert Scowcroft of High Barn Farm, Harwood. Both John and Mary Jane Scowcroft were eighteen years old on their marriage at Harwood Christ's Church, after which they lived at Top o'th' Knotts with John working with his father-in-law on the farm.

Elijah Lonsdale died in December 1908 aged only 59 years and was buried in the Longsight Wesleyan graveyard on the 14th of December, leaving his son-in-law John Scowcroft and his wife Mary Jane with the tenancy. Their first born, a son named Elijah had been born in 1897 but had died at the age of two. Two other sons were born, Robert in 1898 and William in 1899 to be followed by daughters Cecelia, Mary Ann, Isabella and Nellie and sons John, Harry, Arthur, Frank and James.

In 1923 John Scowcroft purchased Top o'th' Knotts (West) from the Haslam family, breaking a direct family ownership line that had lasted over three hundred years since Robert Haslam had been left both Top o'th' Knotts farms in 1621 by his stepfather Henry Haworth.

Robert, William and Jim worked on Top o'th' Knotts Farm all their working lives, while John had his own farm in Smithills for a short time before returning to work at home. Both Harry and Arthur took up other occupations. Of the girls, Cecelia the eldest stayed at Top o'th' Knotts Farm nearly all her life.

John Scowcroft died in 1955 after an accidental fall from the barn loft and was buried in Affetside Chapel graveyard on 16th November. His son Bob had pre-deceased him in 1942 aged 44. The farm Top o'th' Knotts (West) was left to his three sons William, John and Jim but unfortunately John died soon after his father in 1955. William had married Jane Orrell of Bradshaw Brow, while Jim had married Marjory Southworth of Harwood, both raising their families at Top o'th' Knotts.

William Scowcroft died in 1968 aged 68 years and was buried in Affetside Chapel graveyard on 10th January. Jim carried on until the decision was made to sell the farm to the Joule family of Top o'th' Knotts (East) in 1973. Jim retired to live in Bromley Cross while Cecelia came back to live in one of the Top o'th' Knotts cottages until her death in 1987.

Top o'th' Knotts (West) in common with Top o'th' Knotts (East) and Hoyles Farm was worked as a dairy farm from the mid-1800s, producing milk for customers in Tonge Moor and Bolton and delivering by horse drawn milk cart. World War II

Figure 55
John & Mary Jane
Scowcroft
at Top o'th' Knotts c1930.

Figure 56
Top o'th' Knotts milk
float with Cecelia &
Isabella Scowcroft c1930.

Figure 57
William & Jane Scowcroft
with their daughter
Margaret:
Top o'th' Knotts c1933.

interrupted this pattern when the local Agricultural Committee ruled that a proportion of their acreage must be turned over to arable farming. This was aimed at producing foodstuffs to compensate the loss of food imports through the activities of German U Boats. Several fields were ploughed up to grow oats, barley, turnips and potatoes. Not having arable farming implements of their own, these were loaned by the Agricultural Committee as well as in some cases, labour, Steam engined threshing was seen once again in the area.

After World War II, the farming practice returned to dairy farming and the old milk float deliveries continued until a motor van took its place in the 1950s. Also about this time the three or four horses were replaced by a tractor, changing the old farming practices forever. Old mowers, rakes and spinners, etc, were modified to be tractor towed until tractor powered direct drive implements took their place. Milking machines were now in use.

Water was always a problem in the locality and the farms relied on wells and ponds; these were supplemented by boreholes drilled in the 1960s.

The Top o'th' Knotts Farm (East) in 1900 was in the ownership of James Haslam, by this time 71 years of age, and he must have relied wholly on his 30 year old son James who had married Mary Lee of Yeoman's Farm, Affetside on 21st August, 1895. They lived at Top o'th' Knotts with their sons James and Thomas, and daughter Elizabeth.

One of the first jobs of the new century was to rebuild the access road to Tottington Road, the ancient road through Lower Knotts to Riding Gate having become sunken, waterlogged and restrictive. The 1890 OS Map still shows the ancient road from Riding Gate to Top o'th' Knotts and through to Affetside as the main occupation road while the 1910 OS Map gives the emphasis to the road directly through to Tottington Road.

James Haslam Snr died March 31st, 1912 and was buried in the graveyard of St Maxentius. James Haslam Jnr then aged 43 years ran the farm along with his sons James, Thomas and daughter Elizabeth up to his death in March 1938. Son James was by this time living at Cromptons, the neighbouring Bradshaw farm that he had bought, and was running both farms together. Son Thomas had married and taken a farm at Tyldesley. Their sister Elizabeth had married Edward Joule in 1936, the son of a Bolton butcher who had worked on the farm since 1930. On his marriage Edward came to live and work at Top o'th' Knotts (East).

Edward and Elizabeth Joule leased the farm in 1946 in their name from the Haslam family, of which Elizabeth was a member, finally buying it in 1953. Edward later bought Cromptons from his brother-in-law, James Haslam in 1961

74

Figure 58 Haymaking at Top o'th' Knotts: William and Jane Scowcroft with sister Isabella, brother Jim and two Irish labourers who came over to Harwood for harvest time for several years - c1930.

Figure 59 Scowcroft family haymaking in the field overlooking the Raikes Farm with Hill Farm on the horizon - c1930.

Figure 60 Delivery of feed from Whitehursts, the Bolton millers, to Top o'th' Knotts barn/shippon - c1930

Figure 61 Wedding of Edward Joule to Margaret Eddleston in 1962 with Edward (senior). and Elizabeth Joule. Edward's mother, Elizabeth nee Haslam, took the Haslam family line back to 1600.

and James moved to live at Lower Knotts cottages Nos 91/93. These cottages had been left by Robert Haslam (1758-1845) to James's great grandfather, Peter Haslam in 1845.

Edward and Elizabeth Joule had two sons, Edward (b 1936) and James (b 1939), who eventually worked with their father on the joint Cromptons and Top o'th' Knotts (East) farms. They also had one daughter, Mary (b 1941).

The Joule's domestic water supply was pumped up to the house by a windmill powered pump from a collecting tank near the bottom of the field on the westerly side of the lane to Tottington Road. When electric power came up to the area in 1926, the pump was converted to electricity and the windmill became obsolete.

When neighbour Jim Scowcroft decided to retire, the Scowcroft family sold their Top o'th' Knotts (West) farm to Edward Joule in the early 1970s and Edward and Elizabeth Joule moved into the larger Top o'th' Knotts' house.

The summer of 1976 was very dry, particularly for these higher hill farms still relying on local supplies of water from wells and reservoirs. An accidental fire started in Top o'th' Knotts (West) barn destroying thousands of bales of hay as well as the ancient barn itself. The adjacent cottages were also put at risk and the elderly residents, Mrs. Jane Scowcroft and Mrs. Cissie Shuttleworth, were temporarily moved out with their furniture. The local water supply proved to be completely inadequate for fire fighting and water had to be pumped about 1.5 miles from the lodge at the rear of Bradshaw Church by several fire engines parked at intervals up Tottington Road acting as pumping stations. Needless to say by the time the water reached Top o'th' Knotts, the barn and its contents were totally destroyed. The fire had been started by an electrical fault.

Edward Joule died in 1978 and his wife shortly afterwards in 1982. Their eldest son Edward had married Margaret Eddleston in 1962 and although living at Cromptons, took the lead in running it along with the two Top o'th' Knotts farms. His younger brother James had recently married Lynn Gerrard in 1974 and lived at the larger Top o'th' Knotts farm house. Their sister Mary had moved away on marriage and died in 1998.

The last of the Scowcrofts left the two cottages at Top o'th' Knotts when Cecelia died in 1987 and Jane moved into a retirement home. Both cottages were bought by James Joule who by the end of the century had taken over both Top o'th' Knotts farms for cattle grazing. Cromptons farm was sold as a private residence in 1997 with a few acres and Edward moved to High Barn Farm on the other side of Tottington Road which had been bought in 1980. He and his son Paul continue the local farming tradition of the family with their dairy farm still producing milk, but nowadays selling in bulk by tanker rather than deliveries to individual customers. The Joule brothers through their mother Elizabeth Haslam's great-grandfather Peter Haslam, being a son of Robert Haslam (1758-1845), retain a direct family line to Robert Haslam who owned both Top o'th' Knotts Farms in 1622.

Hoyles Fold had been leased from 1894 by Alfred Lowe from the other members of the Lowe family. Alfred's wife Margaret had died in 1893 and was buried in St Maxentius graveyard on October 7th, leaving sons Alfred, John, Thomas, James and Andrew. The family ran their own affairs in a most business-like manner and a lease was drawn up legally and signed by all five brothers. Fixtures, fittings and farm stock were valued as at mother's death with Alfred paying his brothers back their shares and paying £70 per year rent.

Alfred's lease also contained the normal agricultural type conditions stipulating a limit on sale of hay off the farm to 184.5 cubic yards each year and all muck made had to be spread back on the land - this was to preserve the quality of the land for the future. Alfred Lowe continued farming at Hoyles well over his initial seven year lease and was there in 1911 while his brother Andrew farmed at Bradshaw Head, another 'Lowe' farm bought in the 1890s. Andrew Lowe's son Harry was killed at Gallipoli in 1915. Andrew's other son James (b1894) married Jane Ellen Fairclough of Birches Farm, Bradshaw in 1920 and took over Hoyles Fold Farm on Alfred's death. This pattern of family ownership of both Hoyles Fold and Bradshaw Head by the Lowe family continues to the present day.

Hoyles Fold Farm was run on the same lines as the other Knotts Farm, a dairy farm with a milking herd of cows producing milk sold and delivered to the suburbs of North Bolton by a horse drawn milk float, They had three to four heavy horses to draw their implements and carts. The meadows were cut for hay, which could take several weeks to make in bad weather. The hay making process was labour intensive with much hand raking, cocking and finally loaded loose onto carts, to be either stacked outside in haystacks or stored in the barn. This hay was used as winter-feed for the cows and horses which were kept inside over winter. The muck produced was spread by hand over the fields in spring, hopefully in the cold spells when the ground was hard enough to withstand heavy horse and cart traffic. Up to post World War II this was the only means of improving the nutritional value of the grass/hay before the nitrogen and other artificial fertilisers were introduced.

James and Jane Ellen Lowe at Hoyles Fold had a daughter Dorothy born 1926 and son James Jnr in 1927, both attending Affetside School and staying to work on the farm.

Figure 62 James Lowe (senior) in front of farm porch, c1940.

Figure 63 Marriage of John Calderbank to Dorothy Lowe, 1948.

Figure 64 Jim Lowe (junior) on left and Jack Calderbank on right with pair of horses ready for harrowing, c1950.

World War II saw Hoyles Fold having to plough up a few fields to satisfy the local War Agricultural Committee and grow some root crops and oats. This pattern was soon reversed after the war ended. In the 1950s the early Fordson Tractors began to replace the horses for implement and cart drawing while a van was used on the milk round instead of the horse drawn float.

In 1948 Dorothy Lowe married a young man newly demobbed from the RAF named Jack Calderbank and he, with his brother-in-law, Jim Lowe Jnr., continued to work with James Lowe, the father, before his semi-retirement around 1950. Jack and Dorothy Calderbank continued to run Hoyles Fold while Jim Lowe Jnr. married and bought Holts Farm in Turton.

After the death of Fred and Stanley, sons of the late Andrew Lowe, their farm, Bradshaw Head, was put up for auction in 1966 by the family. It was bought jointly by James Lowe Jnr. and his sister Dorothy Calderbank. Jim Lowe Snr. died in 1968; his widow moved to live in a Tottington Road cottage and died in 1976.

Larger acreages became necessary for economic production of milk and beef and to meet this requirement Jack Calderbank bought Castle Farm on the other side of Tottington Road in the late 1950s. Unfortunately, Jack's wife Dorothy died in 1972 and he continued to work the three farms of Hoyles, Bradshaw Head and Castle with their son John (b 1948). They were probably the last of the local farms to have a milk round, which they discontinued in 1997. John, helped by his son Alec, now concentrates on beef production. Five generations of Calderbank/Lowes have farmed at Hoyles.

Over the last fifty years our local farming has changed from labour intensive holdings of 30 to 50 acres each employing several members of the family plus hired help - visiting Irish workers came over year after year at hay time - to holdings now of over 100 acres. The additional acreages came by merging with adjacent farms. These larger holdings are managed by one or two men supplemented by contracting in expensive equipment, such as heavy hay balers and rollers. Some silage is made locally but generally hay is still preferred although the large rolls of 'haylage', wrapped in black polythene are becoming a more common sight in the Knotts area.

Figure 65 Aerial view of Riding Gate and Tottington Road c1950. Note Brookfold Quarry and Hill Farm.

Figure 66
Edge Nook on Tottington Rd:
note Ox Shutt Gate Farm
below - 1988

Figure 67
Edge Nook Cottages on
Tottington Rd: note old
cottages & barn below -1984

Figure 68 Pensford Court
development on the area
previously covered by barn
& cottage above - 2002

Chapteer IX   RIDING GATE AREA   1900-2000

When Harwood and Bradshaw were transferred to the new Turton Urban District Council in 1898, the roads under the Public Health Acts, became the responsibility of the TUDC. Tottington Road, (formerly known as Raikes Lane and earlier Boason's Hill Highway) as a Public Highway established by the Enclosure Act, was re-kerbed and built up in sets.

Riding Gate Lane had been a private occupation road only and in 1902 was adopted by the TUDC. This road ran for approximately 281 yards up to the bridge across Riding Gate Brook adjacent to Nos 59/61 Riding Gate. The cost was recovered from the owners of the frontages. It was probable that at this time the bridge was rebuilt, but it later had to be reconstructed after the great floods of 1927.

The old Riding Gate hamlet on the north side of the brook had entered the 20th Century little changed from 1800 but somewhat neglected. The property on the stream bank in front of No 67 had been demolished leaving a wide occupation lane. One of the early changes would have been the modernising of No 73, increasing its roof height and adding a more modern style of frontage.

For the next sixty to seventy years there were virtually no changes and the 'City' cottages remained very much an artist's delight and were the subject of many paintings. After the First World War this hamlet had become a country retreat for the well-to-do of Bolton and became popular as 'weekend cottages'. The cottages began to be sold rather than remain rented tenancies and consequently there was a fairly regular movement of families to, within and from Riding Gate. The exception to this pattern is the Entwistle/Parton family of No 59 who have lived there for over 100 years.

Provision of services in the 20th Century encouraged both existing and new tenants/owners to improve and extend their homes and progressively from the 1920s more modern developments were installed. Gas had been available from the beginning of the century while electricity came to the area in the 1920s. Mains water supply came to Riding Gate at about the same time although the main sewer came later in 1940. Services to the outlying properties of Raikes and Lower Knotts came much later but they were fully served by the late 1980s.

Preferring older properties, but wanting and being able to afford improved living conditions, owners combined smaller cottages into larger houses as well as building extensions. An early example was the Nook, now 211 Tottington Road, which was originally built as a pair of cottages in 1816 by John Haslam and converted into a single home in the 1950s by builder, Charles Halliday. The front was completely rebuilt but fortunately the date-stone was preserved. John Cole, the owner also built a large garage on the land adjacent to the cottage on Tottington Road for his commercial vehicles. This garage was in turn converted into a separate residence in the 1980s.

Another example of conversion was at Top o'th' Greaves when the two/three cottages were combined into one residence by the Seftons in 1961 and 1973. Also at Lower Knotts, Nos 91 and 93 were combined into one property and a substantial extension was built on to No 83.

Improvement/alterations continued with most of the other cottages on the north side of the brook but fortunately the 'old world' charm of the old Riding Gate hamlet has been preserved. The only intrusions are the motorcar and several garages built on the bank of the stream.

Coming over the brook into the Riding Gate Lane area the pattern of renovation of the older properties has also continued and fortunately their external appearances have been largely preserved.

The first 20th Century housing to be built were the bungalows and a pair of semi-detached Nos 38/40/2/4/6 erected in the 1920s. The bungalows were originally built as wooden chalet type houses and were rebuilt in brickwork a few years later. These were soon followed by the building of three pairs of semi-detached houses, Nos 1 to 11 Riding Gate near the Tottington Road junction in 1933 by Cooper & Daniels, two Bradshaw joiners and builders.

In 1948 Rose Bank was occupied by Fred & Ivy Walton who had moved from Affetside with their market garden business. Of their two acres, one was under glass where they grew tomatoes and flowers, etc, selling first through wholesalers but later selling direct from a stall on Bolton Market. They retired from market gardening in the late 1970s and part of their land along with land to the rear of the old Britannia was later developed with modern housing. A new access road was made on to Riding Gate Lane.

About this time a bungalow was also built on the junction of Brookbottom Lane with Riding Gate Lane.

Up to World War II there were no changes on the Tottington Road area of Riding Gate apart from the demolition of cottages between the old barn and Nos 195-201 in the 1930s. After the War the old style 'ribbon' development continued with the building of Nos 237-253 along Tottington Road above the old Britannia in the late 1960s.

Figure 69 Harwood Primitive Methodists: established 1841 after many years of worship in local cottages.

Figure 70 The present Primitive Methodist Church (rebuilt 1890), with Church Hall to rear and car park forward -2002

Figure 71 The Grey Mare Inn in 1982: it was developed from a cottage beer-house: note horse in field to rear, compare with Figure 30.

Figure 72 The Nook in 2002, having been converted into one house: compare with Figure 32.

Figure 73 The old Britannia Inn, now a private house: note cottages below - 1999.

Figure 74 The Knowles group of cottages - 1992.

Figure 75 Riding Gate Lane with the 1933 houses, looking towards New Green - 2002.

Figure 76 New Green Cottages with the three storey buildings to the right - 2002.

Figure 77
Rose Bank c1960.

Figure 78
Greenhouses of Rose Bank
land c1960

Figure 79
Fred and Ivy Walton.
at work with their market
garden c 1960.

Figure 80 Old Green Cottages - 1975

Figure 81 New Green Terrace - 2002.

Figure 82 The brookside cottages -2002

Figure 83 Entrance to 'Old' Riding Gate, north of the brook - 1980.

The early sixties saw much development of private housing in both Bradshaw and Harwood particularly the nearby New Heys estate. The demand for houses in the area continued and although the local Planning Authority controlled development more tightly there has been continuing pressure to 'fill in' undeveloped areas of the conurbation. Examples have already been noted off Riding Gate Lane up to the old Britannia. Attention turned to the open area between New Green, Top o'th' Brow and the new estate houses of Seaford Road which was eventually developed in 1974/5 as Riding Gate Mews.

By the ruling of the Boundaries Commission in 1974 the old TUDC was broken up with the southern part including Bradshaw and Harwood becoming part of Bolton Metropolitan Borough who, under the powers of the 1971 Town and Country Planning Act, established a number of Conservation Areas. The Riding Gate Conservation Area was established on January 5th, 1976 which included the area bounded by Top o'th' Knotts, across the open land of New Heys Delph to the northwest boundary of New Heys Estate, Riding Gate Mews, down Tottington Road to Oxshutt Gate Farm, the Grey Mare, Tottington Road Methodist Church, Hill Farm and back across to Top o'th' Knotts.

Conservation Area Control limits modern development and may have the beneficial effect of protecting the Green Belt Boundary to the north, east and south of the Riding Gate area.

New houses were built in the 1980s on an 'in-fill' basis, one adjacent to Britannia House and one adjacent to No 253 Tottington Road while the latest group development was the building of the Pensford Court properties in 1986/7. To allow the project it was necessary to demolish the old redundant barn and associated buildings on the area adjacent to Tottington Road bounded by the Edge Nook cottages and Seaford Road to the rear. It is interesting to note that the last Riding Gate shop fell victim in this demolition, the previous one being Mrs. Rush's shop at the end of New Green Terrace.

Notwithstanding Conservation Area Control, the Planning Control Department has condoned the dereliction and final destruction of the Hill Farm buildings due to encroachment of quarrying from nearby Brookfold Quarry.

The last new house in Riding Gate in the 20th Century was the building of Holly Hedge on the site of the recently demolished Mission Hall in 1993.

BIBLIOGRAPHY

Victoria County History of Lancashire.
Enclosure of Harwood Common Act 1797.
Scowcroft Diaries - 1812-1907.
Wills - Lancashire Record Office.
Mining Plans - Bolton Local Studies and Archives.
Lever/Haslam Muniments - 1595-1886 - John Calderbank.
Bradshaw and Harwood Collieries - J J Francis - 1982.
Enclosure of Harwood Commons - J J Francis, 1990.

ACKNOWLEDGEMENTS

Although much information has been gained from Public Records, this work would not have been possible without access to privately held photographs, documents, deeds and locally held knowledge of the area. Thanks are due to the following contributors;

Joan & Jim Ball, New Green, Harwood.
Jean & Eric Broadstock, Riding Gate, Harwood.
John Calderbank, Hoyles Fold Farm, Harwood.
Edwin Coope, Old Green, Harwood.
Jean Gerrard, Lower Knotts, Harwood.
Rev. J and J Gilbert, Turton.
Dr. Leslie Hardman, Lower Knotts, Harwood.
Paul Hartigan, Tottington Road, Harwood.
Dr Kevin Jones, Britannia House, Harwood.
Edward Joule, High Barn Farm, Harwood.
James Joule, Top o'th' Knotts, Harwood.
Jill & David Knott, Knowles Buildings, Harwood.
Margaret & Harold Lindsay, Tottington Road, Harwood.
Jean & Eric Mather, Riding Gate, Harwood.
Ernest Parton. Riding Gate, Harwood.
Mrs A Roberts, Bromley Cross.
Margaret Standish (nee Scowcroft), Bolton.
Jim Scowcroft, Bromley Cross.